The Law Of Attraction

William Walker Atkinson

SANAGE
PUBLISHING HOUSE

Paperback: 978-939-0896-72-1

Any references to historical events, real people, or real places are used fictitiously. Names, characters, and places are products of the author's imagination.

Printed by:
Sanage Publishing House LLP
Mumbai, India
sanagepublishing@gmail.com

Designed by:
allpublishingsolution.com

CONTENTS

PART — 1

THE LAW OF ATTRACTION IN THE THOUGHT WORLD

PART — II

PRACTICAL MENTAL INFLUENCE

ABOUT THE BOOK

In a memorable article of December, 1901 issue of the popular magazine New Thought, the newly appointed editor, William Walker Atkinson, introduced himself to the readers of that periodical in his own words. That article is the crystallised expression of the world principles and the truths which Atkinson's written work illuminates. It contained a crisp, distinct and well—defined statement of his individual creed and it offers a deeper insight into the character and inner self of the man, the author of this book.

In our opinion it should be read by every student of his works, as the key to the philosophy he teaches. It is for this reason that the most vital of the fundamental beliefs enunciated by Mr. Atkinson in that famous introductory statement of 1901 has been prefixed to this book, his latest published title, 'My Working Creed'. Every time one reads the recurring, ringing 'I Believe' by this author, they experience an answering thrill of exaltation and power. To those who read this book I would say, imbue yourself thoroughly with the broad and beautiful spirit of those few preliminary paragraphs that you may pass on understandingly to the perusal of the teachings which follow.

One must definitely read the article from which this Creed is taken as it sheds light on the earlier years of William Walker Atkinson marked by his work, the material success, followed by overstrain, physical and mental breakdown and financial disaster. It shows how he came to know what he now holds to be the truth, and how he has demonstrated its value in his own life. Through these principles, Atkinson had moved from mental and physical wreck and financial ruin towards perfect health, mental vigor and material prosperity.

During the many years of his connection with the magazine, New Thought, Atkinson, built an enduring place for himself in the hearts of its readers. His literary work was confined to its pages (including in addition, three books for its publishers) for four years as article after article of wonderful strength and vital force flowed from his pen. It was during this time that several series of 'lessons' appeared under varying titles, all addressing the application of the Law of Attraction in the Thought World. These lessons created a sensation in the lives of those who applied their principles and exerted a wonderful influence upon them. They were shorn of all atmosphere of the study, all attempt at 'fine writing,' polished periods or dignified metaphor, and all affectation or assumption of superior learning. Mr. Atkinson's sparkling, intimate writing style teemed with thought, force, energy and fire. One of Mr. Atkinson's cardinal principles is 'Stand on your own feet,' and he disapproves any attempt to read infallibility into his writings.

FOREWORD

In which the author has a word to say about 'teachers' and 'discipleshimself included.

I am in receipt of a letter from an earnest student of New Thought, who writes me that he is endeavoring to put into practice the teachings for which I stand. That is all right—I think he will get some good out of the practice (I know that I do). But here is where the trouble comes in—he goes on to say that he is 'a faithful disciple' of mine, and is content to 'sit at the feet of the Teacher.' Now, if you will pardon the slang, I must say that such talk 'makes me tired.' I wish no 'disciples'—disciples are mere parrots repeating what one says—mere human sheep trotting along after some conceited old bell-wether. I do not wish to pose as a bell-wether, nor do I wish a flock of human sheep trotting after me. I want everyone of my fellow students of Mental Science to be his own bell-wether. I like comradeship and mutual help—the help of interdependence. But I don't like this talk of master and disciple—of leader and follower—this talk and idea of dependence.

As for sitting at anyone's feet, the idea arouses all the spirit of independence within me. I don't want to sit at any one's feet—and I don't want any one to sit at mine. I am willing, and often glad, to listen to some teacher and to pick from his teachings such bits of truth as my mind is ready to receive. I am willing to say 'I don't know,' and to accept from others that which appeals to me as truth; not because the other says that it is truth, but because my mind recognizes it as such. I take my own wherever I find it, because I recognize it as mine. I know that all students and teachers get their knowledge from the only source of supply—they can't get it from anywhere else. And if some other fellow happens to see a particular bit of truth before I do, I gladly accept a portion of it from his hands, be he king or beggar; while if I happen to see the thing first, I will gladly share it with all who are ready for it, and who may want it, without feeling that I am a 'leader,' or 'teacher,' or that they are 'followers' or 'disciples.' We are all fellow students—that's all. I recognize no man as my master—and I spurn the person who would call me 'Master,' if there be any so foolish. This feet- sitting talk makes me very, very weary.

I am fully aware that certain teachers convey the idea that they are chosen mouthpieces of the Infinite, and that all true teachings must bear their hall-mark. And I also know the fanatical devotion and bigotry that many of the followers of such teachers manifest. But this is all child's play. The teachers sooner or later will be brought up against good hard stone walls, and their heads will be bruised until they realize 'just where they are at.' And the 'disciples' will have some individuality knocked into them later on, and will be made to stand upon their own feet, by reason of the props being knocked from under them. The New Thought aims at making individuals, not at converting people into droves of sheep, following the tinkle of the bell of some conceited old bell-wether, who imagines that he is the Whole Thing.

The growing soul must realize that it has within itself all that it requires. It may gladly accept from others suggestions, advice, bits of knowledge, and the like, as it goes along—the soul itself being the only judge of what it requires at each particular stage. But, in the end, it must do its own work, and must stand on its own feet. All the teachings in the world will not help you, unless you take hold of the matter yourself and work out your own salvation. You cannot get true mental or spiritual teaching by simply paying so much for a course of lessons, and doing nothing yourself.

You must bring something to the teacher before you can take anything away. You must work up to an understanding before the teachings of another will do you any good.

The teacher may make a suggestion that will open up a line of thought for you, or he may point out a way that has proved of value to him; and thus save you much time and trouble. But you must do the real work yourself.

A teacher may be so filled with the truth that he will overflow, and you will get some of the overflow. I believe that truth is 'catching.' But even so, unless you make that truth your own by living it out, and applying it to your needs, it will do you no good. And so long as you are content to 'sit at his feet,' and do the 'disciple' act, you will not grow one inch. You will be merely a reflection of the teacher, instead of being an individual.

We need a jogging up on this point every once in a while, 'lest we forget.' It is so easy to have your thoughts predigested for you by some teacher or writer—so easy to receive your teaching in capsules. It is so nice to be able to sit down and swallow the tabloid that the teacher or writer kindly has prepared for you, and imagine that you are getting the real thing. But I tell you, friends—it won't do the work. Imbibe all the teachings you please, but you have got to get down to business yourself. You can't give some one else a power of attorney to do the work in your place. Life accepts no substitutes—you must step out yourself. It is mighty easy—this idea of paying so much, in time or money, to some teacher or writer, and then sneaking into the Kingdom of Heaven holding on to his skirts—but it won't work. You've got to do some hustling on your own account, and don't you make any mistake about this fact.

Many of you are running around after teachers, preachers, prophets, seers, 'illuminated souls,' and what not, expecting that your little fee for courses of lessons, private teachings, and all the rest, is going to land you right up in the front rank. Don't you believe a word of it. You've got to go through the motions yourself, before you will attain anything. You can't sneak in that way—it won't work. I look around me and see many of these poor creatures 'sitting at the feet' of some one or other, sinking their individuality in that of the teacher, and not daring to think an original thought—lest it conflict with some notion of their 'Master.' These good souls are so full of the teaching they are imbibing, they will repeat it by the yard, phrase after phrase, like a well-trained parrot. But they don't understand a bit of it. They are like the moon which shines by reason of the reflection of the sun's rays, and has no light or heat of its own. The talk of these 'disciples' and 'sitters-at-the-feet' is nothing but moonshine—mere reflected light. Moons are dead, cold things—no light—no heat—no fire—no energy. Dead, dead, dead—cold, barren and 'played-out.' Stop this moon business and build yourself up into a Sun. You have it in you—manifest it. Start yourself in motion, and manifest Life. Don't suppose that you must be able to solve all the Riddles of the Universe before you can do anything. Never mind about those riddles, just you get down to the task that lies ahead of you, and throw into it some of that

Great Life Principle that is within you waiting for a chance to manifest itself. Don't make the mistake of supposing that this or that teacher has solved the Great Riddle. If he says he has, he is only bluffing and whistling to keep up courage. He may have found a good-sized chunk of the truth, and if he is willing to pass you a bit of it, all right, but he hasn't the Whole Thing, by a mighty sight. The Whole Thing isn't placing itself in the exclusive control of any little bit of itself. No one has a monopoly of knowing—a comer on the Truth. It is yours as much as anybody's—but you must dig for it.

Don't bother about the theories, or the unsolvable riddles—just get down to business and begin to Live. Sometimes I amuse myself by reading some of the theories and 'explanations' of those who think that they have hold of the Whole Thing. After I get through with the theories of one 'dead-sure' chap, I take up the directly opposite theories of another fellow who considers himself the special mouthpiece of the Absolute. Whew! it's a great brain-shaker. If you're not careful you will find yourself being served a nice dish of scrambled brains. When I get sort of 'stewed-up' over such things I go out into the sun and fall back on the 'Laughing Philosophy,' which soon brings me around all right. Nothing will puncture these bubbles so quickly as a good dose of Laughter. Laughter is the only thing that keeps the race from madness. The sense of humor is God's best gift to Man. Try it the next time you get 'stewed up' with 'high statements,' 'basic truths,' 'axiomatic principles.' Beware of any teachings that will not stand the test of the sunny out-of-doors, and the application of the Laughing Philosophy. Shun the teachings that require a pursed-up mouth, and a strained, preternaturally sober face. Have nothing to do with teachings that require a dim, dark, sunless room to be absorbed in—beware of teachings and doctrines that bear the musty smell of the cell upon them. Carry out into the sun the teachings that are offered you, and see whether or not they fade—apply the chemical of laughter, and ascertain whether the stuff bleaches. Remember this test when you are perplexed or worried over some strange theory or doctrine—no matter from whence it comes. If anyone tells you that which will not bear the test—discard the teaching, for it is spurious in that event. Try this on my writings along with the others.

Stop being moons. Stop living by reflected light. Get into action and convert yourself into a living sun. You can do it. It is within your power. Every human soul contains within it the elements of the Sun—get to work and express yourself. Stiffen up your backbone and hold your head erect.

Don't be afraid to say 'I am it.' This is a straight-from-the- shoulder talk. Don't tell me that you are 'disciples' of mine—I disown you; I refuse to have disciples. Don't try to 'sit at my feet'—if you do, I will use my feet to push you off the platform. I need room to swing my feet about and don't want people sitting there. But if you wish to call me 'Brother,' or 'Fellow Student,' or 'Schoolmate in the Kindergarten of God,' I will be glad to have you do so. That's all we are, after all—little babes tugging away at the breast of the Absolute.

—William Walker Atkinson.

MY WORKING CREED

The 'I believe' of the author.

I believe that the mind of Man contains the greatest of all forces—that Thought is one of the greatest manifestations of energy.

I believe that the man who understands the use of Thought-force can make of himself practically what he will.

I believe that not only is one's body subject to the control of the mind, but that, also, one may change environment, 'luck,' circumstances, by positive thought taking the place of negative. I know that the 'I Can and I Will' attitude will carry one forward to Success that will seem miraculous to the man on the 'I Can't' plane.

I believe that 'thoughts are things,' and that the Law of Attraction in the thought world will draw to one just what he desires or fears.

I believe in the gospel of work—in 'hustling.' I believe in the I do, as well as the I am. I know that the man who will take advantage of the Power of the Mind, and who will manifest that power in action, will go forward to Success as surely and as steadily as the arrow from the bow of the skilled archer.

I believe in the Brotherhood of Man. I believe in being Kind.

I believe in everyone minding his own business—and allowing everyone else the same privilege. I believe that we have no right to condemn—'let him who is without sin cast the first stone.' I believe that he who Hates is an assassin; that he who Covets is a thief; that he who Lusts is an adulterer; that the gist of a crime is in its desire. Seeing this—looking into our own hearts—how can we condemn? I believe that Evil is but Ignorance.

I believe that 'to know all is to forgive all.' I believe that there is good in every man; let us help him to manifest it.

I believe in the absolute equality of the Man and the Woman—sometimes I think that the odds are slightly in favor of the Woman.

I believe in the sacredness of Sex—but I also believe that Sex manifests on the Spiritual and Mental planes as well as on the Physical. And I believe that to the pure all things are pure.

I believe that man is immortal—that the Real Self is Spirit, which uses mind and body as its tools, and manifests itself according to the fitness of the tools.

I believe that Man is rapidly growing into a new plane of consciousness, in which he will know himself as he is—will recognize the I am—the Something Within.

I believe that there is an Infinite Power in, and of, all things.

I believe that, although today we have but the faintest idea of that Power, still we will steadily grow to comprehend it more fully—will get in closer touch with it. Even now we have momentary glimpses of its existence—a momentary consciousness of Oneness with the Absolute.

I believe that the greatest happiness consists in maintaining toward the Absolute the attitude of the trusting child, who, feeling no doubt of the parent's love—no doubt of his wisdom—places his little hand in that of the parent, and says 'Lead Thou me on.' I believe that he who feels towards the Absolute, the trustfulness of the babe which places its little tired head close to the breast of the mother, will also be conscious of the tender answering pressure, as the babe is drawn just a little closer to the mother-heart.

—William Walker Atkinson

PART – 1

THE LAW OF ATTRACTION IN THE THOUGHT WORLD

CHAPTER 1

THE LAW OF ATTRACTION IN THE THOUGHT WORLD

One great Law—Thought a manifestation of Energy—Thought Vibration—Vibrations of light and heat differ solely in rate of vibration—Human brain only instrument capable of registering thought-waves—Experiments in telepathy prove the law of thought-attraction—Like attracts like in the Thought-world—The wireless telegraphy of the mind—A field of energy with established laws.

The Universe is governed by Law—one great Law. Its manifestations are multiform, but viewed from the Ultimate there is but one Law. We are familiar with some of its manifestations, but are almost totally ignorant of certain others. Still we are learning a little more every day—the veil is being gradually lifted.

We speak learnedly of the Law of Gravitation, but ignore that equally wonderful manifestation, The Law of Attraction in the Thought World. We are familiar with that wonderful manifestation of Law which draws and holds together the atoms of which matter is composed—we recognize the power of the law that attracts bodies to the earth, that holds the circling worlds in their places, but we close our eyes to the mighty law that draws to us the things we desire or fear, that makes or mars our lives.

When we come to see that Thought is a force—a manifestation of energy—having a magnet-like power of attraction, we will begin to understand the why and wherefore of many things that have heretofore seemed dark to us. There is no study that will so well repay the student for his time and trouble as the study of the workings of this mighty law of the world of Thought—the Law of Attraction.

When we think we send out vibrations of a fine ethereal substance, which are as real as the vibrations manifesting light, heat, electricity, magnetism. That these vibrations are not evident to our five senses is no proof that they do not exist. A powerful magnet will send out vibrations and exert a force sufficient to attract to itself a piece of steel weighing a hundred pounds, but we can neither see, taste, smell, hear nor feel the mighty force. These thought vibrations, likewise, cannot be seen, tasted, smelled, heard nor felt in the ordinary way; although it is true there are on record cases of persons peculiarly sensitive to psychic impressions who have perceived powerful thought- waves, and very many of us can testify that we have distinctly felt the thought vibrations of others, both whilst in the presence of the sender and at a distance. Telepathy and its kindred phenomena are not idle dreams.

Light and heat are manifested by vibrations of a far lower intensity than those of Thought, but the difference is solely in the rate of vibration. The annals of science throw an interesting light upon this question. Prof. Elisha Gray, an eminent scientist, says in his little book, 'The Miracles of Nature':

'There is much food for speculation in the thought that there exist sound-waves that no human ear can hear, and color-waves of light that no eye can see. The long, dark, soundless space between 40,000 and 400,000,000,000,000 vibrations per second, and the infinity of range beyond 700,000,000,000,000 vibrations per second, where light ceases, in the universe of motion, makes it possible to indulge in speculation. '

M. M. Williams, in his work entitled 'Short Chapters in Science,' says: 'There is no gradation between the most rapid undulations or tremblings that produce our sensation of sound, and the slowest of those which give rise to our sensations of gentlest warmth. There is a huge gap between them, wide enough to include another world of motion, all lying between our world of sound and our world of heat and light; and there is no good reason whatever for supposing that matter is incapable of such intermediate activity, or that such activity may not give rise to intermediate sensations, provided there are organs for taking up and sensifying their movements.'

I cite the above authorities merely to give you food for thought, not to attempt to demonstrate to you the fact that thought vibrations exist. The last-named fact has been fully established to the satisfaction of numerous investigators of the subject, and a little reflection will show you that it coincides with your own experiences.

We often hear repeated the well-known Mental Science statement, 'Thoughts are Things,' and we say these words over without consciously realizing just what is the meaning of the statement. If we fully comprehended the truth of the statement and the natural consequences of the truth back of it, we should understand many things which have appeared dark to us, and would be able to use the wonderful power, Thought Force, just as we use any other manifestation of Energy.

As I have said, when we think we set into motion vibrations of a very high degree, 'but just as real as the vibrations of light, heat, sound, electricity.' And when we understand the laws governing the production and transmission of these vibrations we will be able to use them in our daily life, just as we do the better known forms of energy. That we cannot see, hear, weigh or measure these vibrations is no proof that they do not exist. There exist waves of sound which no human ear can hear, although some of these are undoubtedly registered by the ear of some of the insects, and others are caught by delicate scientific instruments invented by man; yet there is a great gap between the sounds registered by the most delicate instrument and the limit which man's mind, reasoning by analogy, knows to be the boundary line between sound-waves and some other forms of vibration. And there are light waves which the eye of man does not register, some of which may be detected by more delicate instruments, and many more so fine that the instrument has not yet been invented which will detect them, although improvements are being made every year and the unexplored field gradually lessened.

As new instruments are invented, new vibrations are registered by them—and yet the vibrations were just as real before the invention of the instrument as afterward. Supposing that we had no instruments to register magnetism—one might be justified in denying the existence of that mighty force, because it could not be tasted, felt, smelt, heard, seen, weighed or measured. And yet the mighty magnet would still send out waves of force sufficient to draw to it pieces of steel weighing hundreds of pounds. Each form of vibration requires its own form of instrument for registration. At present the human brain seems to be the only instrument capable of registering thought waves, although occultists say that in this century scientists will invent apparatus sufficiently delicate to catch and register such impressions. And from present indications it looks as if the invention named might be expected at any time. The demand exists and undoubtedly will be soon supplied. But to those who have experimented along the lines of practical telepathy no further proof is required than the results of their own experiments.

We are sending out thoughts of greater or less intensity all the time, and we are reaping the results of such thoughts. Not only do our thought-waves influence ourselves and others, but they have a drawing power—they attract to us the thoughts of others, things, circumstances, people, 'luck,' in accord with the character of the thought uppermost in our minds. Thoughts of Love will attract to us the Love of others; circumstances and surroundings in accord with the thought; people who are of like thought. Thoughts of Anger, Hate, Envy, Malice and Jealousy will draw to us the foul brood of kindred thoughts emanating from the minds of others; circumstances in which we will be called upon to manifest these vile thoughts and will receive them in turn from others; people who will manifest in harmony; and so on.

A strong thought, or a thought long continued, will make us the center of attraction for the corresponding thought-waves of others. Like attracts like in the Thought World—as ye sow so shall ye reap. Birds of a feather flock together in the Thought World—curses like chickens come home to roost, and bring their friends with them.

The man or woman who is filled with Love sees Love on all sides and attracts the Love of others. The man with Hate in his heart gets all the Hate he can stand. The man who thinks Fight generally runs up against all the Fight he wants before he gets through. And so it goes, each gets what he calls for over the wireless telegraphy of the Mind. The man who rises in the morning feeling 'grumpy' usually manages to have the whole family in the same mood before the breakfast is over. The 'nagging' woman generally finds enough to gratify her 'nagging' propensity during the day.

This matter of Thought Attraction is a serious one. When you stop to think of it you will see that a man really makes his own surroundings, although he blames others for it. I have known people who understood this law to hold a positive, calm thought and be absolutely unaffected by the in harmony surrounding them. They were like the vessel from which the oil had been poured on the troubled waters—they rested safely and calmly whilst the tempest raged around them. One is not at the mercy of the fitful storms of Thought after he has learned the workings of the Law.

We have passed through the age of physical force on to the age of intellectual supremacy, and are now entering a new and almost unknown field, that of psychic power. This field of energy has its established laws, as well as have the others, and we should acquaint ourselves with them or we will be crowded to the wall as are the ignorant on the planes of effort. I will endeavor to make plain to you the great underlying principles of this new field of energy which is opening up before us, that you may be able to make use of this great power and apply it for legitimate and worthy purposes, just as men are using steam, electricity and other forms of energy today.

CHAPTER 2

THOUGHT WAVES AND THEIR PROCESS OF REPRODUCTION

How thought-waves traverse the sea of Mind—The power possessed of reproducing themselves—Vibrations which affect us—Those which do not—Why?—We are what we have thought ourselves into being—The agency of others' thoughts in shaping our destiny—The working of the Law of Attraction illustrated by the Marconi wireless instruments—The Mind has many degrees of pitch—Positive thought—Negative thought—We are positive to some, negative to others—A knowledge of Mental Law can change us from negative to positive—More people on negative plane than on positive plane—Consequently more negative thought-vibrations—How to counterbalance them—Affirmations and auto-suggestions, and their uses—Establishing new mental attitudes—Development of the Will—A high tension not at all times desirable—Advantage of changing from positive to receptive, at will.

Like a stone thrown into the water, thought produces ripples and waves which spread out over the great ocean of thought. There is this difference, however: the waves on the water move only on a level plane in all directions, whereas thought-waves move in all directions from a common center, just as do the rays from the sun.

Just as we here on earth are surrounded by a great sea of air, so are we surrounded by a great sea of Mind. Our thought-waves move through this vast mental ether, extending, however, in all directions, as I have explained, becoming somewhat lessenedin intensity according to the distance traversed, because of the friction occasioned by the waves coming in contact with the great body of Mind surrounding us on all sides.

These thought-waves have other qualities differing from the waves on the water. They have the property of reproducing themselves. In this respect they resemble sound-waves rather than waves upon the water. Just as a note of the violin will cause the thin glass to vibrate and 'sing,' so will a strong thought tend to awaken similar vibrations in minds attuned to receive it. Many of the 'stray thoughts' which come to us are but reflections or answering vibrations to some strong thought sent out by another. But unless our minds are attuned to receive it, the thought will not likely affect us. If we are thinking high and great thoughts, our minds acquire a certain keynote corresponding to the character of the thoughts we have been thinking. And, this keynote once established, we will be apt to catch the vibrations of other minds keyed to the same thought. On the other hand, let us get into the habit of thinking thoughts of an opposite character, and we will soon be echoing the low order of thought emanating from the minds of the thousands thinking along the same lines.

We are largely what we have thought ourselves into being, the balance being represented by the character of the suggestions and thought of others, which have reached us either directly by verbal suggestions or telepathically by means of such thought- waves. Our general mental attitude, however, determines the character of the thought-waves received from others as well as the thoughts emanating from ourselves. We receive only such thoughts as are in harmony with the general mental attitude held by ourselves; the thoughts not in hannony affecting us very little, as they awaken no response in us.

The man who believes thoroughly in himself and maintains a positive strong mental attitude of Confidence and Determination is not likely to be affected by the adverse and negative thoughts of Discouragement and Failure emanating from the minds of other persons in whom these last qualities predominate. At the same time these negative thoughts, if they reach one whose mental attitude is pitched on a low key, deepen his negative state and add fuel to the fire which is consuming his strength, or, if you prefer this figure, serve to further smother the fire of his energy and activity.

We attract to us the thoughts of others of the same order of thought. The man who thinks success will be apt to get into tune with the minds of others thinking likewise, and they will help him, and he them. The man who allows his mind to dwell constantly upon thoughts of failure brings himself into close touch with the minds of other 'failure' people, and each will tend to pull the other down still more. The man who thinks that all is evil is apt to see much evil, and will be brought into contact with others who will seem to prove his theory. And the man who looks for good in everything and everybody will be likely to attract to himself the things and people corresponding to his thought. We generally see that for which we look.

You will be able to carry this idea more clearly if you will think of the Marconi wireless instruments, which receive the vibrations only from the sending instrument which has been attuned to the same key, while other telegrams are passing through the air in near vicinity without affecting the instrument. The same law applies to the operations of thought. We receive only that which corresponds to our mental attunement. If we have been discouraged, we may rest assured that we have dropped into a negative key, and have been affected not only by our own thoughts but have also received the added depressing thoughts of similar character which are constantly being sent out from the minds of other unfortunates who have not yet learned the law of attraction in the thought world. And if we occasionally rise to heights of enthusiasm and energy, how quickly we feel the inflow of the courageous, daring, energetic, positive thoughts being sent out by the live men and women of the world. We recognize this without much trouble when we come in personal contact with people and feel their vibrations, depressing or invigorating, as the case may be. But the same law operates when we are not in their presence, although less strongly.

The mind has many degrees of pitch, ranging from the highest positive note to the lowest negative note, with many "notes in between, varying in pitch according to their respective distance from the positive or negative extreme.When your mind is operating along positive lines you feel strong, buoyant, bright, cheerful, happy, confident and courageous, and are enabled to do your work well, to carry out your intentions, and progress on your road to Success. You send out strong positive thought, which affects others and causes them to co-operate with you or to follow your lead, according to their own mental keynote.

When you are playing on the extreme negative end of the mental keyboard you feel depressed, weak, passive, dull, fearful, cowardly. And you find yourself unable to make progress or to succeed. And your effect upon others is practically nil. You are led by, rather than leading others, and are used as a human doormat or football by more positive persons.

In some persons the positive element seems to predominate; and in others the negative quality seems to be more in evidence. There are, of course, widely varying degrees of positiveness and negativeness, and b may be negative to a, while positive to c. When two people first meet there is generally a silent mental conflict in which their respective minds test their quality of positiveness, and fix their relative position toward each other. This process may be unconscious in many cases, but it occurs nevertheless. The adjustment is often automatic, but occasionally the struggle is so sharp—the opponents being so well matched—that the matter forces itself into the consciousness of the two people. Sometimes both parties are so much alike in their degrees of positiveness that they practically fail to come to terms, mentally; they never really are able to get along with each other, and they are either mutually repelled and separate or else stay together amid constant broils and wrangling.

We are positive or negative to everyone with whom we have relations. We may be positive to our children, our employees and dependents, but we are at the same time negative to others to whom we occupy inferior positions, or whom we have allowed to assert themselves over us.

Of course, something may occur and we will suddenly become more positive than the man or woman to whom we have heretofore been negative. We frequently see cases of this kind. And as the knowledge of these mental laws becomes more general we will see many more instances of persons asserting themselves and making use of their new-found power.

But remember you possess the power to raise the keynote of your mind to a positive pitch by an effort of the will. And, of course, it is equally true that you may allow yourself to drop into a low, negative note by carelessness or a weak will.

There are more people on the negative plane of thought than on the positive plane, and consequently there are more negative thought vibrations in operation in our mental atmosphere. But, happily for us, this is counterbalanced by the fact that a positive thought is infinitely more powerful than a negative one, and if by force of will we raise ourselves to a higher mental key we can shut out the depressing thoughts and may take up the vibrations corresponding with our changed mental attitude. This is one of the secrets of the affirmations and auto-suggestions used by the several schools of Mental Science and other New Thought cults. There is no particular merit in affirmations of themselves, but they serve a twofold purpose: (1) They tend to establish new mental attitudes within us and act wonderfully in the direction of character building—the science of making ourselves over. (2) They tend to raise the mental keynote so that we may get the benefit of the positive thought-waves of others on the same plane of thought.

Whether or not we believe in them, we are constantly making affirmations. The man who asserts that he can and will do a thing—

and asserts it earnestly—develops in himself the qualities conducive to the well doing of that thing, and at the same time places his mind in the proper key to receive all the thought-waves likely to help him in the doing. If, on the other hand, one says and feels that he is going to fail, he will choke and smother the thoughts coming from his own subconscious mentality which are intended to help him, and at the same time will place himself in tune with the Failure—thought of the world—and there is plenty of the latter kind of thought around, I can tell you.

Do not allow yourselves to be affected by the adverse and negative thoughts of those around you. Rise to the upper chambers of your mental dwelling, and key yourself up to a strong pitch, away above the vibrations on the lower planes of thought. Then you will not only be immune to their negative vibrations but will be in touch with the great body of strong positive thought coming from those of your own plane of development.

My aim will be to direct and train you in the proper use of thought and will, that you may have yourself well in hand and may be able to strike the positive key at any moment you may feel it necessary. It is not necessary to strike the extreme note on all occasions. The better plan is to keep yourself in a comfortable key, without much strain, and to have the means at command whereby you can raise the pitch at once when occasion demands. By this knowledge you will not be at the mercy of the old automatic action of the mind, but may have it well under your own control.

Development of the will is very much like the development of a muscle—a matter of practice and gradual improvement. At first it is apt to be tiresome, but at each trial one grows stronger until the new strength becomes real and permanent. Many of us have made ourselves positive under sudden calls or emergencies. We are in the habit of 'bracing up' when occasion demands. But by intelligent practice you will be so much strengthened that your habitual state will be equal to your 'bracing up' stage now, and then when you find it necessary to apply the spur you will be able to reach a stage not dreamed of at present.

Do not understand me as advocating a high tension continuously. This is not at all desirable, not only because it is apt to be too much of a strain upon you but also because you will find it desirable to relieve the tension at times and become receptive that you may absorb impressions. It is well to be able to relax and assume a certain degree of receptiveness, knowing that you are always able to spring back to the more positive state at will. The habitually strongly positive man loses much enjoyment and recreation. Positive, you give out expressions; receptive, you take in impressions. Positive, you are a teacher; receptive, a pupil. It is not only a good thing to be a good teacher, but it is also very important to be a good listener at times.

CHAPTER 3

A TALK ABOUT THE MIND

Man has but one Mind—Functions along two lines of mental effort—Passive effort often result of vibratory impulses imparted in ages long past—Active effort new-born—Thought impulse and motion impulse result of Active effort—Active function creates, Passive function obeys orders and suggestions—Active function sends forth vibrations—The force of Habit—Appetency—The impulse of the Primal Cause—'Life-force'—Mental Culture and Mental Development, two different things—The amenability of the Mind to the Will—The Will the outward manifestation of the I am—The attraction of The Absolute—The real Man the master—Active and Passive functions but tools.

Man has but one mind, but he has many mental faculties, each faculty being capable of functioning along two different lines of mental effort.

There are no distinct dividing lines separating the two several functions of a faculty, but they shade into each other as do the colors of the spectrum.

An Active effort of any faculty of the mind is the result of a direct impulse imparted at the time of the effort. A Passive effort of any faculty of the mind is the result of either a preceding Active effort of the same mind; an Active effort of another along the lines of suggestion; Thought Vibrations from the mind of another; Thought impulses from an ancestor, transmitted by the laws of heredity (including impulses transmitted from generation to generation from the time of the original vibratory impulse imparted by the Primal Cause—which impulses gradually unfold, and unsheath, when the proper state of evolutionary development is reached).

The Active effort is new-born—fresh from the mint, whilst the Passive effort is of less recent creation, and, in fact, is often the result of vibratory impulses imparted in ages long past. The Active effort makes its own way, brushing aside the impeding vines and kicking from its path the obstructing stones. The Passive effort travels along the beaten path.

A thought-impulse, or motion-impulse, originally caused by an Active effort of faculty, may become by continued repetition, or habit, strictly automatic, the impulse given it by the repeated Active effort developing a strong momentum, which carries it on, along Passive lines, until stopped by another Active effort or its direction changed by the same cause.

On the other hand, thought-impulses, or motion-impulses, continued along Passive lines may be terminated or corrected by an Active effort. The Active function creates, changes or destroys. The Passive function carries on the work given it by the Active function and obeys orders and suggestions.

The Active function produces the thought-habit, or motion-habit, and imparts to it the vibrations which carry it on along the Passive lines thereafter. The Active function also has the power to send forth vibrations which neutralize the momentum of the thought-habit, or motion-habit; it also is able to launch a new thought-habit, or motion-habit, with stronger vibrations, which overcomes and absorbs the first thought, or motion, and substitutes the new one.

All thought-impulses, or motion-impulses, once started on their errands, continue to vibrate along passive lines until corrected or terminated by subsequent impulses imparted by the Active function, or other controlling power. The continuance of the original impulse adds momentum and force to it, and renders its correction or tennination more difficult. This explains that which is called 'the force of habit.' I think that this will be readily understood by those who have struggled to overcome a habit which had been easily acquired. The Law applies to good habits as well as bad. The moral is obvious.

Several of the faculties of the mind often combine to produce a single manifestation. A task to be performed may call for the combined exercise of several faculties, some of which may manifest by Active effort and others by Passive effort.

The meeting of new conditions—new problems—calls for the exercise of Active effort; whilst a familiar problem, or task, can be easily handled by the Passive effort without the assistance of his more enterprising brother.

There is in Nature an instinctive tendency of living organisms to perform certain actions, the tendency of an organized body to seek that which satisfies the wants of its organism. This tendency is sometimes called Appetency. It is really a Passive mental impulse, originating with the impetus imparted by the Primal Cause, and transmitted along the lines of evolutionary development, gaining strength and power as it progresses. The impulse of the Primal Cause is assisted by the powerful upward attraction exerted by The Absolute.

In plant life this tendency is plainly discernible, ranging from the lesser exhibitions in the lower types to the greater in the higher types. It is that which is generally spoken of as the 'life force' in plants. It is, however, a manifestation of rudimentary mentation, functioning along the lines of Passive effort. In some of the higher forms of plant life there appears a faint color of independent 'life action'—a faint indication of choice of volition. Writers on plant life relate many remarkable instances of this phenomenon. It is, undoubtedly, an exhibition of rudimentary Active mentation. In the lower animal kingdom a very high degree of Passive mental effort is found. And, varying in degree in the several families and species, a considerable amount of Active mentation is apparent. The lower animal undoubtedly possesses Reason only in a lesser degree than man, and, in fact, the display of volitional mentation exhibited by an intelligent animal is often nearly as high as that shown by the lower types of man or by a young child.

As a child, before birth, shows in its body the stages of the physical evolution of man, so does a child, before and after birth—until maturity—manifest the stages of the mental evolution of man.

Man, the highest type of life yet produced, at least upon this planet, shows the highest form of Passive mentation, and also a much higher development of Active mentation than is seen in the lower animals, and yet the degrees of that power vary widely among the different races of men.

Even among men of our race the different degrees of Active mentation are plainly noticeable; these degrees not depending by any means upon the amount of 'culture,' social position or educational advantages possessed by the individual. Mental Culture and Mental Development are two very different things.

You have but to look around you to see the different stages of the development of Active mentation in man. The reasoning of many men is scarcely more than Passive mentation, exhibiting but little of the qualities of volitional thought. They prefer to let other men think for them. Active mentation tires them and they find the instinctive, automatic, Passive mental process much easier. Their minds work along the lines of least resistance. They are but little more than human sheep.

Among the lower animals and the lower types of men Active mentation is largely confined to the grosser faculties—the more material plane; the higher mental faculties working along the instinctive, automatic lines of the Passive function.

As the lower forms of life progressed in the evolutionary scale, they developed new faculties, which were latent within them. These faculties always manifested in the form of rudimentary Passive functioning, and afterwards worked up,through higher Passive forms, until the Active functions were brought into play. The evolutionary process still continues, the invariable tendency being toward the goal of highly developed Active mentation. This evolutionary progress is caused by the vibratory impulse imparted by the Primal Cause, aided by the uplifting attraction of The Absolute.

This law of evolution is still in progress, and man is beginning to develop new powers of mind, which, of course, are first manifesting themselves along the lines of Passive effort. Some men have developed these new faculties to a considerable degree, and it is possible that before long Man will be able to exercise them along the line of their Active functions. In fact, this power has already been attained by a few. This is the secret of the Oriental occultists, and of some of their Occidental brethren.

The amenability of the mind to the Will can be increased by properly directed practice. That which we are in the habit of referring to as the 'strengthening of the Will' is in reality the training of the mind to recognize and absorb the Power Within. The Will is strong enough; it does not need strengthening, but the mind needs to be trained to receive and act upon the suggestions of the Will. The Will is the outward manifestation of the I am. The Will current is flowing in full strength along the spiritual wires; but you must learn how to raise the trolley-pole to touch it before the mental car will move. This is a somewhat different idea from that which you have been in the habit of receiving from writers on the subject of Will Power, but it is correct, as you will demonstrate to your own satisfaction if you will follow up the subject by experiments along the proper lines.

The attraction of The Absolute is drawing man upward, and the vibratory force of the Primal Impulse has not yet exhausted itself. The time of evolutionary development has come when man can help himself. The man who understands the Law can accomplish wonders by means of the development of the powers of the mind; whilst the man who turns his back upon the truth will suffer from his lack of knowledge of the Law.

He who understands the laws of his mental being, develops his latent powers and uses them intelligently. He does not despise his Passive mental functions, but makes good use of them also, charges them with the duties for which they are best fitted, and is able to obtain wonderful results from their work, having mastered them and trained them to do the bidding of the Higher Self. When they fail to do their work properly he regulates them, and his knowledge prevents him from meddling with them unintelligently, and thereby doing himself harm. He develops the faculties and powers latent within him and learns how to manifest them along the line of Active mentation as well as Passive. He knows that the real man within him is the master to whom both Active and Passive functions are but tools. He has banished Fear, and enjoys Freedom. He has found himself. He has learned the secret of the I am.

CHAPTER 4

MIND BUILDING

The Power of Man—Unconscious mind-building—The 'I,' the sovereign of the Mind—The Universal Will—The mastery of the Lower Self—The mental misgoverned by irresponsible faculties—The reestablishment of order in the mental kingdom—The first battle—The conquest of the Lesser Self by the Real Self- Affirmation and exercise.

Man can build up his mind and make it what he wills. In fact, we are mind-building every hour of our lives, either consciously or unconsciously. The majority of us are doing the work unconsciously, but those who have seen a little below the surface of things have taken the matter in hand and have become conscious creators of their own mentality. They are no longer subject to the suggestions and influences of others but have become masters of themselves. They assert the 'I,' and compel obedience from the subordinate mental faculties. The 'I' is the sovereign of the mind, and what we call will is the instrument of the 'I.' Of course, there is something back of this, and the Universal Will is higher than the Will of the Individual, but the latter is in much closer touch with the Universal Will than is generally supposed, and when one conquers the lower self, and asserts the 'I,' he becomes in close touch with the Universal Will and partakes largely of its wonderful power. The moment one asserts the 'I,' and 'finds himself,' he establishes a close connection between the Individual Will and the Universal Will. But before he is able to avail himself of the mighty power at his' command, he must first effect the Mastery of the lower self.

Think of the absurdity of Man claiming to manifest powers, when he is the slave of the lower parts of his mental being, which should be subordinate. Think of a man being the slave of his moods, passions, animal appetites and lower faculties, and at the same time trying to claim the benefits of the Will. Now, I am not preaching asceticism, which seems to me to be a confession of weakness. I am speaking of Self-Mastery—the assertion of the 'I' over the subordinate parts of oneself. In the higher view of the subject, this 'I' is the only real Self, and the rest is the non-self; but our space does not permit the discussion of this point, and we will use the word 'self ' as meaning the entire man. Before a man can assert the 'I' in its full strength he must obtain the complete mastery of the subordinate parts of the self. All things are good when we learn to master them, but no thing is good when it masters us. Just so long as we allow the lower portions of the self to give us orders, we are slaves. It is only when the 'I' mounts his throne and lifts the sceptre, that order is established and things assume their proper relation to each other.

We are finding no fault with those who are swayed by their lower selves—they are in a lower grade of evolution, and will work up in time. But we are calling the attention of those who are ready, to the fact that the Sovereign must assert his will, and that 'the subjects must obey. Orders must be given and carried out. Rebellion must be put down, and the rightful' authority insisted upon. And the time to do it is Now.

You have been allowing your rebellious subjects to keep the King from his throne. You have been allowing the mental kingdom to be misgoverned by irresponsible faculties. You have been the slaves of Appetite, Unworthy Thoughts, Passion and Negativeness. The Will has been set aside and Low Desire has usurped the throne. It is time to re-establish order in the mental kingdom. You are able to assert the mastery over any emotion, appetite, passion or class of thoughts by the assertion of the Will. You can order Fear to go to the rear; Jealousy to leave your presence; Hate to depart from your sight; Anger to hide itself; Worry to cease troubling you; Uncontrolled Appetite and Passion to bow in submission and to become humble slaves instead of masters—all by the assertion of the 'I.' You may surround yourself with the glorious company of Courage, Love and Self- Control, by the same means. You may put down the rebellion and secure peace and order in your mental kingdom if you will but utter the mandate and insist upon its execution.

Before you march forth to empire, you must establish the proper internal conditions—must show your ability to govern your own kingdom. The first battle is the conquest of the lesser self by the Real Self.

AFFIRMATION

I am Asserting the Mastery of my Real Self

Repeat these words earnestly and positively during the day, at least once an hour, and particularly when you are confronted with conditions which tempt you to act on the lines of the lesser self instead of following the course dictated by the Real Self. In the moment of doubt and hesitation, say these words earnestly, and your way will be made clear to you. Repeat them several times after you retire and settle yourself to sleep. But be sure to back up the words with the thought inspiring them, and do not merely repeat them parrot-like. Form the mental image of the Real Self asserting its mastery over the lower planes of your mind—see the King on his Throne. You will become conscious of an influx of new thought, and things which have seemed hard for you will suddenly become much easier. You will feel that you have yourself well in hand, and that you are the master and not the slave. The thought you are holding will manifest itself in action, and you will steadily grow to become that which you have in mind.

Exercise

Fix the mind firmly on the higher Self and draw inspiration from it when you feel led to yield to the promptings of the lower part of your nature. When you are tempted to burst into Anger—assert the 'I,' and your voice will drop. Anger is unworthy of the developed Self. When you feel vexed and cross, remember what you are, and rise above your feeling. When you feel Fearful, remember that the Real Self fears nothing, and assert Courage. When you feel Jealousy inciting, think of your higher nature, and laugh. And so on, asserting the Real Self and not allowing the things on the lower plane of mentality to disturb you. They are unworthy of you, and must be taught to keep their places. Do not allow these things to master you—they should be your subjects, not your masters. You must get away from this plane, and the only way to do so is to cut loose from these phases of thought which have been 'running things' to suit themselves. You may have trouble at the start, but keep at it and you will have that satisfaction which comes only from conquering the lower parts of our nature. You have been a slave long enough—now is the time to free yourselves. If you will follow these exercises faithfully you will be a different being by the end of the year, and will look back with a pitying smile to your former condition. But it takes work. This is not child's play, but a task for earnest men and women. Will you make the effort?

CHAPTER 5

THE SECRET OF THE WILL

The Will Power and its capability of being developed, disciplined, controlled and directed—Every man the possessor, potentially, of a strong will—The great power-house of the Universal Will Power—Will does not need training, but Mind does—Mind, the instrument—Menially lazy people—Strong will follows strong desire—The price of attainment—The real test-The secret of the development of the Will—Auto-suggestion and exercise.

While psychologists may differ in their theories regarding the nature of the Will, none deny its existence, nor question its power. All persons recognize the power of strong Will—all see how it may be used to overcome the greatest obstacles. But few realize that the Will may be developed and strengthened by intelligent practice. They feel that they could accomplish wonders if they had a strong Will, but instead of attempting to develop it, they content themselves with vain regrets. They sigh, but do nothing.

Those who have investigated the subject closely know that Will Power, with all its latent possibilities and mighty powers, may be developed, disciplined, controlled and directed, just as may be any other of Nature's forces. It does not matter what theory you may entertain about the nature of the Will, you will obtain the results if you practice intelligently.

Personally, I have a somewhat odd theory about the Will. I believe that every man has, potentially, a strong Will, and that all he has to do is to train his mind to make use of it. I think that in the higher regions of the mind of every man is a great store of Will Power awaiting his use. The Will current is running along the psychic wires, and all that it is necessary to do is to raise the mental trolley-pole and bring down the power for your use. And the supply is unlimited, for your little storage battery is connected with the great power house of the Universal Will Power, and the power is inexhaustible. Your Will does not need training—but your Mind does. The mind is the instrument and the supply of Will Power is proportionate to the fineness of the instrument through which it manifests. But you needn't accept this theory if you don't like it. This lesson will fit your theory as well as mine.

He who has developed his mind so that it will allow the Will Power to manifest through it, has opened up wonderful possibilities for himself. Not only has he found a great power at his command, but he is able to bring into play, and use, faculties, talents and abilities of whose existence he has not dreamed. This secret of the Will is the magic key which opens all doors.

The late Donald G. Mitchell once wrote: 'Resolve is what makes a man manifest; not puny resolve, but crude determination; not errant purpose—but that strong and indefatigable will which treads down difficulties and danger, as a boy treads down the heaving frost-lands of winter; which kindles his eye and brain with a proud pulse-beat toward the unattainable. Will makes men giants.' Many of us feel that if we would but exert our Will, we might accomplish wonders. But somehow we do not seem to want to take the trouble—at any rate, we do not get to the actual willing point. We put it off from time to time, and talk vaguely of 'some day,' but that some day never comes.

We instinctively feel the power of the Will, but we haven't enough energy to exercise it, and so drift along with the tide, unless perhaps some friendly difficulty arises, some helpful obstacle appears in our path, or some kindly pain stirs us into action, in either of which cases we are compelled to assert our Will and thus begin to accomplish something.

The trouble with us is that we do not want to do the thing enough to make us exert our Will Power. We don't want to hard enough. We are mentally lazy and of weak Desire. If you donot like the word Desire substitute for it the word 'Aspiration.' (Some people call the lower impulses Desires, and the higher, Aspirations—it's all a matter of words, take your choice.) That is the trouble. Let a man be in danger of losing his life—let a woman be in danger of losing a great love—and you will witness a startling exhibition of Will Power from an unexpected source. Let a woman's child be threatened with danger, and she will manifest a degree of Courage and Will that sweeps all before it. And yet the same woman will quail before a domineering husband, and will lack the Will to perform a simple task. A boy will do all sorts of work if he but considers it play, and yet he can scarcely force himself to cut a little fire-wood. Strong Will follows strong Desire. If you really want to do a thing very much, you can usually develop the Will Power to accomplish it.

The trouble is that you have not really wanted to do these things, and yet you blame your Will. You say that you do want to do it, but if you stop to think you will see that you really want to do something else more than the thing in question. You are not willing to pay the price of attainment. Stop a moment and analyze this statement and apply it to your own case.

You are mentally lazy—that's the trouble. Don't talk to me about not having enough Will. You have a great storehouse of Will awaiting your use, but you are too lazy to use it. Now, if you are really in earnest about this matter, get to work and first find out what you really want to do—then start to work and do it. Never mind about the Will Power—you'll find a full supply of that whenever you need it. The thing to do is to get to the point where you will resolve to Will. That's the real test—the resolving. Think of these things a little, and make up your mind whether or not you really want to be a Wilier sufficiently hard to get to work.

Many excellent essays and books have been written on this subject, all of which agree regarding the greatness of Will Power, the most enthusiastic terms being used; but few have anything to say about how this power may be acquired by those who have it not, or who possess it in but a limited degree. Some have given exercises designed to 'strengthen' the Will, which exercises really strengthen the Mind so that it is able to draw upon its store of power. But they have generally overlooked the fact that in autosuggestion is to be found the secret of the development of the mind so that it may become the efficient instrument of the Will.

AUTO-SUGGESTION

I am Using my Will Power

Say these words several times earnestly and positively, immediately after finishing this article.

Then repeat them frequently during the day, at least once an hour, and particularly when you meet something that calls for the exercise of Will Power. Also repeat them several times after you retire and settle yourself for sleep. Now, there is nothing in these words unless you back them up with the thought. In fact, the thought is 'the whole thing,' and the words only pegs upon which to hang the thought. So think of what you are saying, and mean, what you say. You must use Faith at the start, and use the words with a confident expectation of the result. Hold the steady thought that you are drawing on your storehouse of Will Power, and before long you will find that thought is taking form in action, and that your Will Power is manifesting itself. You will feel an influx of strength with each repetition of the words. You will find yourself overcoming difficulties and bad habits, and will be surprised at how things are being smoothed out for you.

Exercise

Perform at least one disagreeable task each day during the month. If there is any specially disagreeable task which you would like to shirk, that is the one for you to perform. This is not given you in order to make you self-sacrificing or meek, or anything of that sort—it is given you to exercise your Will. Anyone can do a pleasant thing cheerfully, but it takes Will to do the unpleasant thing cheerfully; and that is how you must do the work. It will prove a most valuable discipline to you. Try it for a month and you will see where it 'comes in.' If you shirk this exercise you had better stop right here and acknowledge that you do not want Will Power, and are content to stay where you are and remain a weakling.

CHAPTER 6

HOW TO BECOME IMMUNE TO INJURIOUS THOUGHT ATTRACTION

The first thing to do—Fear thought—Strong expectancy a powerful magnet—The man who fears—How to overcome the habit of Fear—A waste of time to fight negative thought by denying it—The right mental attitude—Setting new vibrations in motion—The conquest of Fear the first important step—The positive will prevail.

The first thing to do is to begin to 'cut out' Fear and Worry. Fear thought is the cause of much unhappiness and many failures. You have been told this thing over and over again, but it will bear repeating. Fear is a habit of mind which has been fastened upon us by negative race-thought, but from which we may free ourselves by individual effort and perseverance.

Strong expectancy is a powerful magnet. He of the strong, confident desire attracts to him the things best calculated to aid him—persons, things, circumstances, surroundings; if he desires them hopefully, trustfully, confidently, calmly. And, equally true, he who Fears a thing generally manages to start into operation forces which will cause the thing he feared to come upon him.

Don't you see, the man who Fears really expects the feared thing, and in the eyes of the Law it is the same as if he really had wished for or desired it? The Law is operative in both cases—the principle is the same.

The best way to overcome the habit of Fear is to assume the mental attitude of Courage, just as the best way to get rid of darkness is to let in the light. It is a waste of time to fight a negative thought-habit by recognizing its force and trying to deny it out of existence by mighty efforts. The best, surest, easiest and quickest method is to assume the existence of the positive thought desired in its place; and by constantly dwelling upon the positive thought, manifest it into objective reality. Therefore, instead of repeating, 'I'm not afraid,' say boldly, 'I am full of Courage,' 'I am Courageous.' You must assert, 'There's nothing to fear,' which, although in the nature of a denial, simply denies the reality of the object causing fear rather than admitting the fear itself and then denying it.

To overcome Fear, one should hold firmly to the mental attitude of Courage. He should think Courage, say Courage, act Courage. He should keep the mental picture of Courage before him all the time, until it becomes his normal mental attitude. Hold the ideal firmly before you and you will gradually grow to its attainment—the ideal will become manifest.

Let the word 'Courage" sink deeply into your mind, and then hold it firmly there until the mind fastens it in place. Think of yourself as being Courageous—see yourself as acting with Courage in trying situations. Realize that there is nothing to Fear—that Worry and Fear never helped anyone, and never will. Realize that Fear paralyzes effort, and that Courage promotes activity. The confident, fearless, expectant, 'I Can and I Will' man is a mighty magnet. He attracts to himself just what is needed for his success. Things seem to come his way, and people say he is 'lucky.' Nonsense! 'Luck' has nothing to do with it. It's all in the Mental Attitude. And the Mental Attitude of the 'I Can't' or the 'I'm Afraid' man also determines his measure of success. There's no mystery whatsoever about it. You have but to look about you to realize the truth of what I have said. Did you ever know a successful man who did not have the 'I Can and I Will' thought strong within him? Why, he will walk all around the 'I Can't' man, who has perhaps even more ability.

The first mental attitude brought to the surface latent qualities, as well as attracted help from outside; whilst the second mental attitude not only attracted 'I Can't' people and things, but also kept the man's own powers from manifesting themselves. I have demonstrated the correctness of these views, and so have many others, and the number of people who know these things is growing every day.

Don't waste your Thought-Force, but use it to advantage. Stop attracting to yourself failure, unhappiness, in harmony, sorrow—begin now and send out a current of bright, positive, happy thought. Let your prevailing thought be 'I Can and I Will;' think 'I Can and I Will;' dream T Can and I Will;' say 'I Can and I Will;' act 'I Can and I Will.' Live on the 'I Can and I Will' plane, and before you are aware of it, you will feel the new vibrations manifesting themselves in action; will see them bring results; will be conscious of the new point of view; will realize that your own is coming to you. You will feel better, act better, see better, be better in every way, after you join the T Can and I Will' brigade.

Fear is the parent of Worry, Hate, Jealousy, Malice, Anger, Discontent, Failure and all the rest. The man who rids himself of Fear will find that the rest of the brood have disappeared. The only way to be Free is to get rid of Fear. Tear it out by the roots. I regard the conquest of Fear as the first important step to be taken by those who wish to master the application of Thought Force. So long as Fear masters you, you are in no condition to make progress in the realm of Thought, and I must insist that you start to work at once to get rid of this obstruction. You can do it—if you only go about it in earnest. And when you have ridded yourself of the vile thing, life will seem entirely different to you—you will feel happier, freer, stronger, more positive, and will be more successful in every undertaking of Life.

Start in today, make up your mind that this intruder must go—do not compromise matters with him, but insist upon an absolute surrender on his part. You will find the task difficult at first, but each time you oppose him he will grow weaker, and you will be stronger. Shut off his nourishment—starve him to death—he cannot live in a thought—atmosphere of Fearlessness. So, start to fill your mind with good, strong, Fearless thoughts—keep yourself busy thinking Fearlessness, and Fear will die of his own accord. Fearlessness is positive—Fear is negative, and you may be sure that the positive will prevail.

So long as Fear is around with his 'but,' 'if,' 'suppose,' 'I'm afraid,' 'I can't,' 'what if,' and all the rest of his cowardly suggestions, you will not be able to use your Thought Force to the best advantage. Once get him out of the way, you will have clear sailing, and every inch of thought-sail will catch the wind. He is a Jonah. Overboard with him! (The whale who swallows him will have my sympathy.) I advise that you start in to do some of the things which you feel you could do if you were not afraid to try. Start to work to do these things, affirming 'Courage' all the way through, and you will be surprised to see how the changed mental attitude will clear away obstacles from your path, and will make things very much easier than you had anticipated. Exercises of this kind will develop you wonderfully, and you will be much gratified at the result of a little practice along these lines.

There are many things before you awaiting accomplishment, which you can master if you will only throw aside the yoke of Fear—if you will only refuse to accept the race suggestion, and will boldly assert the 'I' and its power. And the best way to vanquish Fear is to assert 'Courage' and stop thinking of Fear. By this plan you will train the mind into new habits of thought, thus eradicating the old negative thoughts which have been pulling you down, and holding you back. Take the word 'Courage' with you as your watchword and manifest it in action.

Remember, the only thing to fear is Fear, and—well, don't even fear Fear, for he's a cowardly chap at the best, who will run if you show a brave front.

CHAPTER 7

THE TRANSMUTATION OF NEGATIVE THOUGHT

Worry the child of Fear—The motive underlying action The causes that result in Success How Desire acts—Worry negative and death-producing—Desire and Ambition positive and life- producing—The transmutation of Worry—Getting into harmony with the right thought-waves—Setting in motion the Law of Attraction—Fear paralyzes Desire—Once rid of it, difficulty melts away—The working of a mighty Law—The things we worry about—Things adjust themselves—The storing-up of energy Where are the feared things?—Better ways of overcoming objectionable thoughts than by fighting them.

Worry is the child of Fear—if you kill out Fear, Worry will die for want of nourishment. This advice is very old, and yet it is always worthy of repetition, for it is a lesson of which we are greatly in need. Some people think that if we kill out Fear and Worry we will never be able to accomplish anything. I have read editorials in the great journals in which the writers held that without Worry one can never accomplish any of the great tasks of life, because Worry is necessary to stimulate interest and work. This is nonsense, no matter who utters it. Worry never helped one to accomplish anything; on the contrary, it stands in the way of accomplishment and attainment. The motive underlying action and 'doing things' is Desire and Interest. If one earnestly desires a thing, he naturally becomes very much interested in its accomplishment, and is quick to seize upon anything likely to help him to gain the thing he wants. More than that, his mind starts up a work on the sub-conscious plane that brings into the field of consciousness many ideas of value and importance. Desire and Interest are the causes that result in success. Worry is not Desire. It is true that if one's surroundings and environments become intolerable, he is driven in desperation to some efforts that will result in throwing off the undesirable conditions and in the acquiring of those more in harmony with his desire. But this is only another form of Desire—the man desires something different from what he has; and when his desire becomes strong enough his entire interest is given to the task, he makes a mighty effort, and the change is accomplished. But it wasn't Worry that caused the effort. Worry could content itself with wringing its hands and moaning 'Woe is me,' and wearing its nerves to a frazzle, and accomplishing nothing. Desire acts differently. It grows stronger as the man's conditions become intolerable, and finally when he feels the hurt so strongly that he can't stand it any longer, he says, 'I won't stand this any longer—I will make a change,' and lo! then Desire springs into action. The man keeps on 'wanting' a change the worst way (which is the best way) and his Interest and Attention being given to the task of deliverance, he begins to make things move. Worry never accomplished anything. Worry is negative and death producing. Desire and Ambition are positive and life producing. A man may worry himself to death and yet nothing will be accomplished, but let that man transmute his worry and discontent into Desire and Interest, coupled with a belief that he is able to make the change—the 'I Can and I Will' idea—then something happens.

Yes, Fear and Worry must go before we can do much. One must proceed to cast out these negative intruders, and replace them with Confidence and Hope. Transmute Worry into keen Desire. Then you will find that Interest is awakened, and you will begin to think things of interest to you. Thoughts will come to you from the great reserve stock in your mind and you will start to manifest them in action. Moreover you will be placing yourself in harmony with similar thoughts of others, and will draw to you aid and assistance from the great volume of thought waves with which the world is filled. One draws to himself thought waves corresponding in character with the nature of the prevailing thoughts in his own mind—his mental attitude. Then again he begins to set into motion the great Law of Attraction, whereby he draws to him others likely to help him, and is, in turn, attracted to others who can aid him. This Law of Attraction is no joke, no metaphysical absurdity, but is a great live working principle of Nature, as anyone may learn by experimenting and observing.

To succeed in anything you must want it very much—Desire must be in evidence in order to attract. The man of weak desires attracts very little to himself. The stronger the Desire the greater the force set into motion. You must want a thing hard enough before you can get it. You must want it more than you do the things around you, and you must be prepared to pay the price for it. The price is the throwing overboard of certain lesser desires that stand in the way of the accomplishment of the greater one. Comfort, ease, leisure, amusements, and many other things may have to go (not always, though). It all depends on what you want. As a rule, the greater the thing desired, the greater the price to be paid for it. Nature believes in adequate compensation. But if you really Desire a thing in earnest, you will pay the price without question; for the Desire will dwarf the importance of the other things.

You say that you want a thing very much, and are doing everything possible toward its attainment? Pshaw! you are only playing Desire. Do you want the thing as much as a prisoner wants freedom—as much as a dying man wants life? Look at the almost miraculous things accomplished by prisoners desiring freedom. Look how they work through steel plates and stone walls with a bit of stone. Is your desire as strong as that? Do you work for the desired thing as if your life depended upon it? Nonsense! you don't know what Desire is. I tell you if a man wants a thing as much as the prisoner wants freedom, or as much as a strongly vital man wants life, then that man will be able to sweep away obstacles and impediments apparently immovable. The key to attainment is Desire, Confidence, and Will. This key will open many doors.

Fear paralyzes Desire—it scares the life out of it. You must get rid of Fear. There have been times in my life when Fear would get hold of me and take a good, firm grip on my vitals, and I would lose all hope; all interest; all ambition; all desire. But, thank the Lord, I have always managed to throw off the grip of the monster and face my difficulty like a man; and lo! things would seem to be straightened out for me somehow. Either the difficulty would melt away, or I would be given means to overcome it, or get around, or under or over it. It is strange how this works. No matter how great is the difficulty, when we finally face it with courage and confidence in ourselves, we seem to pull through somehow, and then we begin to wonder what we were scared about. This is not a mere fancy, it is the working of a mighty law, which we do not as yet fully understand, but which we may prove at any time.

People often ask: 'It's all very well for you New Thought people to say 'Don't worry,' but what's a person to do when he thinks of all the possible things ahead of him, which might upset him and his plans?' Well, all that I can say is that the man is foolish to bother about thinking of troubles to come at some time in the future. The majority of things that we worry about don't come to pass at all; a large proportion of the others come in a milder form than we had anticipated, and there are always other things which come at the same time which help us to overcome the trouble. The future holds in store for us not only difficulties to be overcome, but also agents to help us in overcoming the difficulties. Things adjust themselves. We are prepared for any trouble which may come upon us, and when the time comes we somehow find ourselves able to meet it. God not only tempers the wind to the shorn lamb, but He also tempers the shorn lamb to the wind. The wind and the shearing do not come together; there is usually enough time for the lamb to get seasoned, and then he generally grows new wool before the cold blast comes.

It has been well said that nine-tenths of the worries are over things which never come to pass, and that the other tenth is over things of little or no account. So what's the use in using up all your reserve force in fretting over future troubles, if this be so? Better wait until your troubles really come before you worry. You will find that by this storing up of energy you will be able to meet about any sort of trouble that comes your way.

What is it that uses up all the energy in the average man or woman, anyway? Is it the real overcoming of difficulties, or the worrying about impending troubles? It's always 'Tomorrow, tomorrow,' and yet tomorrow never comes just as we feared it would. Tomorrow is all right; it carries in its grip good things as well as troubles. Bless my soul, when I sit down and think over the things which I once feared might possibly descend upon me, I laugh! Where are those feared things now? I don't know—have almost forgotten that I ever feared them.

You do not need to fight Worry—that isn't the way to overcome the habit.

Just practice concentration, and then learn to concentrate upon something right before you, and you will find that the worry thought has vanished. The mind can think of but one thing at a time, and if you concentrate upon a bright thing, the other thing will fade away. There are better ways of overcoming objectionable thoughts than by fighting them. Learn to concentrate upon thoughts of an opposite character, and you will have solved the problem.

When the mind is full of worry thoughts, it cannot find time to work out plans to benefit you. But when you have concentrated upon bright, helpful thoughts, you will discover that it will start to work subconsciously; and when the time comes you will find all sorts of plans and methods by which you will be able to meet the demands upon you. Keep your mental attitude right, and all things will be added unto you. There's no sense in worrying; nothing has ever been gained by it, and nothing ever will be. Bright) cheerful and happy thoughts attract bright, cheerful and happy things to us—worry drives them away. Cultivate the right mental attitude.

CHAPTER 8

THE LAW OF MENTAL CONTROL

Thoughts either faithful servants or tyrannical masters—Some of our best mental work performed for us when our conscious mentality is at rest—The key to the mystery—The man who understands how to run his mental engine—'Slowing down' the Mind.

Your thoughts are either faithful servants or tyrannical masters—just as you allow them to be. You have the say about it; take your choice. They will either go about your work under direction of the firm will, doing it the best they know how, not only in your waking hours, but when you are asleep—some of our best mental work being performed for us when our conscious mentality is at rest, as is evidenced by the fact that when the morning comes we find troublesome problems have been worked out for us during the night, after we had dismissed them from our minds —apparently; or they will ride all over us and make us their slaves if we are foolish enough to allow them to do so. More than half the people of the world are slaves of every vagrant thought which may see fit to torment them.

Your mind is given you for your good and for your own use—not to use you. There are very few people who seem to realize this and who understand the art of managing the mind. The key to the mystery is Concentration. A little practice will develop within every man the power to use the mental machine properly. When you have some mental work to do concentrate upon it to the exclusion of everything else, and you will find that the mind will get right down to business-to the work at hand- and matters will be cleared up in no time. There is an absence of friction, and all waste motion or lost power is obviated. Every pound of energy is put to use, and every revolution of the mental driving—wheel counts for something. It pays to be able to be a competent mental engineer.

And the man who understands how to run his mental engine knows that one of the important things is to be able to stop it when the work has been done. He does not keep putting coal in the furnace, and maintaining a high pressure after the work is finished, or when the day's portion of the work has been done, and the fires should be banked until the next day. Some people act as if the engine should be kept running whether there was any work to be done or not, and then they complain if it gets worn out and wobbles and needs repairing. These mental engines are fine machines, and need intelligent care.

To those who are acquainted with the laws of mental control it seems absurd for one to lie awake at night fretting about the problems of the day, or more often, of the morrow. It is just as easy to slow down the mind as it is to slow down an engine, and thousands of people are learning to do this in these days of New Thought. The best way to do it is to think of something else—as far different from the obtruding thought as possible. There is no use fighting an objectionable thought with the purpose of 'downing' it; that is a great waste of energy, and the more you keep on saying, 'I won't think of this thing!' the more it keeps on coming into your mind, for you are holding it there for the purpose of hitting it. Let it go; don't give it another thought; fix the mind on something entirely different, and keep the attention there by an effort of the will. A little practice will do much for you in this direction. There is only room for one thing at a time in the focus of attention; so put all your attention upon one thought, and the others will sneak off. Try it for yourself.

CHAPTER 9

ASSERTING THE LITE FORCE

A general awakening needed—Let Life flow through us, manifesting in thought, word, deed—The expression of conscious life—Affirmation and Exercise.

I have spoken to you of the advantage of getting rid of Fear. Now I wish to put life into you. Many of you have been going along as if you were dead—no ambition—no energy—no vitality—no interest—no life. This will never do. You are stagnating. Wake up and display a few signs of life! This is not the place in which you can stalk around like a living corpse—this is the place for wide-awake, active, live people, and a good general awakening is what is needed; although it would take nothing less than a blast from Gabriel's trumpet to awaken some of the people who are stalking around thinking that they are alive, but who are really dead to all that makes life worth while.

We must let Life flow through us, and allow it to express itself naturally. Do not let the little worries of life, or the big ones either, depress you and cause you to lose your vitality. Assert the Life Force within you, and manifest it in every thought, act and deed, and before long you will be exhilarated and fairly bubbling over with vitality and energy.

Put a little life into your work—into your pleasures—into yourself. Stop doing things in a half-hearted way, and begin to take an interest in what you are doing, saying and thinking. It is astonishing how much interest we may find in the ordinary things of life, if we will only wake up. There are interesting things all around us—interesting events occurring every moment—but we will not be aware of them unless we assert our life force and begin to actually live instead of merely existing.

No man or woman ever amounted to anything unless he or she put life into the tasks of everyday life—the acts—the thoughts. What the world needs is live men and women. Just look into the eyes of the people whom you meet, and see how few of them are really alive. The most of them lack that expression of conscious life which distinguishes the man who lives from the one who simply exists.

I want you to acquire this sense of conscious life so that you may manifest it in your life and show what Mental Science has done for you. I want you to get to work today and begin to make yourselves over according to the latest pattern. You can do this if you will only take the proper interest in the task.

AFFIRMATION AND EXERCISE

'I am Alive'

Fix in your mind the thought that the 'I' within you is very much alive and that you are manifesting life fully, mentally and physically. And keep this thought there, aiding yourself with constant repetitions of the watchword. Don't let the thought escape you, but keep pushing it back into the mind. Keep it before the mental vision as much as possible. Repeat the watchword when you awaken in the morning—say it when you retire at night. And say it at meal times, and whenever else you can during the day—at least once an hour. Form the mental picture of yourself as filled with Life and Energy. Live up to it as far as possible. When you start in to perform a task say 'IAm Alive' and mix up as much life as possible in the task. If you find yourself feeling depressed, say 'I Am Alive,' and then take a few deep breaths, and with each inhalation let the mind hold the thought that you are breathing in Strength and Life, and as you exhale, hold the thought that you are breathing out all the old, dead, negative conditions and are glad to get rid of them. Then finish up with an earnest, vigorous affirmation: 'I Am Alive,' and mean it when you say it, too.

And let your thoughts take form in action. Don't rest content with merely saying that you are alive, but prove it with your acts. Take an interest in doing things, and don't go around 'mooning' or day-dreaming. Get down to business, and live.

CHAPTER 10

TRAINING THE HABIT MIND

The sub-conscious mind—Importance of transmitting proper impulses—Automatic habits—'Which of these two things shall I do?'—Forming a new habit—Breaking an old one—The Just- once' idea—The Mind a piece of paper—Mental creases.

Professor William James, the well-known teacher of, and writer upon Psychology, very truly says: 'The great thing in all education is to make our nervous system our ally instead of our enemy. For this we must make automatic and habitual, as early as possible, as many useful actions as we can, and as carefully guard against growing into ways that are likely to be disadvantageous. In the acquisition of a new habit, or the leaving off of an old one, we must take care to launch ourselves with as strong and decided initiative as possible. Never suffer an exception to occur until the new habit is securely rooted in your life. Seize the very first possible opportunity to act on every resolution you make and on every emotional prompting you may experience, in the direction of the habits you aspire to gain.' This advice is along the lines familiar to all students of Mental Science, but it states the matter more plainly than the majority of us have done. It impresses upon us the importance of passing on to the subconscious mind the proper impulses, so that they will become automatic and 'second nature.' Our subconscious mentality is a great store house for all sorts of suggestions from ourselves and others, and, as it is the 'habit-mind,' we must be careful to send it the proper material from which it may make habits. If we get into the habit of doing certain things, we may be sure that the subconscious mentality will make it easier for us to do just the same thing over and over again, easier each time, until finally we are firmly bound with the ropes and chains of the habit, and find it more or less difficult, sometimes almost impossible, to free ourselves from the hateful thing.

We should cultivate good habits against the hour of need. The time will come when we will be required to put forth our best efforts, and it rests with us today whether that hour of need shall find us doing the proper thing automatically and almost without thought, or struggling to do it bound down and hindered with the chains of things opposed to that which we desire at that moment.

We must be on guard at all times to prevent the forming of undesirable habits. There may be no special harm in doing a certain thing today, or perhaps again tomorrow, but there may be much harm in setting up the habit of doing that particular thing. If you are confronted with the question: 'Which of these two things should I do?' the best answer is: 'I will do that which I would like to become a habit with me.' In forming a new habit, or in breaking an old one, we should throw ourselves into the task with as much enthusiasm as possible, in order to gain the most ground before the energy expends itself when it meets with friction from the opposing habits already formed. We should start in by making as strong an impression as possible upon the subconscious mentality. Then we should be constantly on guard against temptations to break the new resolution 'just this once.' This 'just once' idea kills off more good resolutions than any other one cause. The moment you yield 'just this once,' you introduce the thin edge of the wedge that will, in the end, split your resolution into pieces.

Equally important is the fact that each time you resist temptation the stronger does your resolution become. Act upon your resolution as early and as often as possible, as with every manifestation of thought in action, the stronger does it become. You are adding to the strength of your original resolution every time you back it up with action.

The mind has been likened to a piece of paper that has been folded. Ever afterwards it has a tendency to fold in the same crease—unless we make a new crease or fold, when it will follow the last lines. And the creases are habits-every time we make one it is so much easier for the mind to fold along the same crease afterward. Let us make our mental creases in the right direction.

CHAPTER 11

THE PSYCHOLOGY OF EMOTION

Emotions dependent largely upon habit—May be repressed, increased, developed, changed—When to master an undesirable emotion—Jealousy—Its growth—Rage—The habit of feeling and acting 'mean '—Worry—Continued thought manifests in action—'Fault-finding'—The chronic 'nagger'—Negative emotions and their recurrence—How to choke out these habits.

One is apt to think of the emotions as independent from habit. We easily may think of one acquiring habits of action, and even of thinking, but we are apt to regard the emotions as something connected with 'feeling' and quite divorced from intellectual effort. Yet, notwithstanding the distinction between the two, both are dependent largely upon habit, and one may repress, increase, develop, and change one's emotions, just as one may regulate habits of action and lines of thought. It is an axiom of psychology that 'Emotions deepen by repetition.' If a person allows a state of feeling to thoroughly take possession of him, he will find it easier to yield to the same emotion the second time, and so on, until the particular emotion or feeling becomes second nature to him. If an undesirable emotion shows itself inclined to take up a permanent abode with you, you had better start to work to get rid of it, or at least to master it.

And the best time to do this is at the start; for each repetition renders the habit more firmly intrench'ed, and the task of dislodging it more difficult.

Were you ever jealous? If so, you will remember how insidious was its first approach, how subtly it whispered hateful suggestions into your willing ear, and how gradually it followed up such suggestions, until, finally you began to see green, (Jealousy has an effect upon the bile, and causes it to poison the blood. This is why the idea of green is always associated with it.) Then you will remember how the thing seemed to grow, taking possession of you until you scarcely could shake it off. You found it much easier to become jealous the next time. It seemed to bring before you all sorts of objects apparently justifying your suspicions and feeling. Everything began to look green—the green-eyed monster waxed fat.

And so it is with every feeling or emotion. If you give way to a fit of rage, you will find it easier to become angry the next time, on less provocation. The habit of feeling and acting 'mean' does not take long to firmly settle itself in its new home if encouraged. Worry is a great habit for growing and waxing fat. People start by worrying about big things, and then begin to worry and fret about some smaller thing. And then the merest trifle worries and distresses them. They imagine that all sorts of evil things are about to befall them. If they start on a journey they are certain there is going to be a wreck. If a telegram comes, it is sure to contain some dreadful tidings.

If a child seems a little quiet, the worrying mother is positive it is going to fall ill and die. If the husband seems thoughtful, as he revolves some business plan in his mind, then the good wife is convinced that he is beginning to cease to love her, and indulges in a crying spell. And so it goes—worry, worry, worry—each indulgence making the habit more at home. After a while the continued thought shows itself in action. Not only is the mind poisoned by the blue thoughts, but the forehead shows deep lines between the eyebrows, and the voice takes on that whining, rasping tone so common among worry- burdened people.

The condition of mind known as 'fault-finding' is another emotion that grows fat with exercise. First, fault is found with this thing, then with that, and finally with everything. The person becomes a chronic 'nagger'—a burden to friends and relatives, and a thing to be avoided by outsiders. Women make the greatest naggers. Not because men are any better, but simply because a man nagger is apt to have the habit knocked out of him by other men who will not stand his nonsense—he finds that he is making things too hot for himself, and he reforms; while a woman has more of a chance to indulge in the habit. But this nagging is all a matter of habit. It grows from small beginnings, and each time it is indulged in it throws out another root, branch, or tendril, and fastens itself the closer to the one who has given it soil in which to grow.

Envy, uncharitableness, gossip, scandal-mongering, are all habits of this kind. The seeds are in every human breast, and only need good soil and a little watering to become lusty and strong.

Each time you give way to one of these negative emotions, the easier do you make it for a recurrence of the same thing, or similar ones. Sometimes by encouraging one unworthy emotion, you find that you have given room for the growth of a whole family of these mental weeds.

Now, this is not a good old orthodox preachment against the sin of bad thoughts. It is merely a calling of your attention to the law underlying the psychology of emotions. Nothing new about it old as the hills—so old that many of us have forgotten all about it.

If you wish to manifest these constantly disagreeable and unpleasant traits, and to suffer the unhappiness that comes from them, by all means do so—that is your own business, and privilege. It's none of mine, and I am not preaching at you—it keeps me busy minding my own business and keeping an eye on my own undesirable habits and actions. I am merely telling you the law regarding the matter, and you may do the rest. If you wish to choke out these habits, there are two ways open to you. First, whenever you find yourself indulging in a negative thought or feeling, take right hold of it and say to it firmly, and vigorously, 'Get out!' It won't like this at first, and will bridle up, curve its back and snarl like an offended cat. But never mind—just say 'Scat' to it. The next time it will not be so confident and aggressive—it will have manifested a little of the fear-habit. Each time you repress and choke out a tendency of this kind, the weaker it will become, and the stronger will your will be.

Professor James says: 'Refuse to express a passion, and it dies. Count ten before venting your anger, and its occasion seems ridiculous. Whistling to keep up courage is no mere figure of speech. On the other hand, sit all day in a moping posture, sigh, and reply to everything with a dismal voice, and your melancholy lingers. There is no more valuable precept in moral education than this, as all who have experience know: if we wish to conquer emotional tendencies in ourselves, we must assiduously, and in the first instance, cold-bloodedly, go through the outward movements of those contrary dispositions which we prefer to cultivate. Smooth the brow, brighten the eye, contract the dorsal rather than the ventral aspect of the frame, and speak in a major key, pass the genial compliment, and your heart must be frigid indeed if it does not gradually thaw.'

CHAPTER 12

DEVELOPING NEW BRAIN CELLS

Undesirable states of feeling—We are not the creatures of our emotions—The majority of the race so governed to a great degree—Man the real master of his emotions—The development of new brain-cells—The disuse of old brain-cells with undesirable manifestations—The brain, the organ and instrument of the Mind—Our tendencies, temperaments and predispositions—The millions of unused brain-cells—Mental attitudes acquired or discarded at will—The mind clears the way for thoughts good for the individual, interposes resistance to those which are harmful—One positive thought will counteract a number of negative thoughts—'Holding the thought'—How to cultivate a certain habit of action—Ridding oneself of a mental trait.

I have spoken of the plan of getting rid of undesirable states of feeling by driving them out. But a far better way is to cultivate the feeling or emotion directly opposed to the one you wish to eradicate.

We are very apt to regard ourselves as the creatures of our emotions and feelings, and to fancy that these feelings and emotions are 'we.' But such is far from being the truth. It is true that the majority of the race are slaves of their emotions and feelings, and are governed by them to a great degree. They think that feelings are things that rule one and from which one cannot free himself, and so they cease to rebel. They yield to the feeling without question, although they may know that the emotion or mental trait is calculated to injure them, and to bring unhappiness and failure instead of happiness and success. They say 'we are made that way,' and let it go at that. The new Psychology is teaching the people better things. It tells them that they are masters of their emotions and feelings, instead of being their slaves. It tells them that brain-cells may be developed that will manifest along desirable lines, and that the old brain-cells that have been manifesting so unpleasantly may be placed on the retired list, and allowed to atrophy from want of use. People may make themselves over, and change their entire natures. This is not mere idle theory, but is a working fact which has been demonstrated by thousands of people, and which is coming more and more before the attention of the race.

No matter what theory of mind we entertain, we must admit that the brain is the organ and instrument of the mind, in our present state of existence, at least, and that the brain must be considered in this matter. The brain is like a wonderful musical instrument, having millions of keys, upon which we may play innumerable combinations of sounds. We come into the world with certain tendencies, temperaments, and predispositions. We may account for these tendencies by heredity, or we may account for them upon theories of pre-existence, but the facts remain the same. Certain keys seem to respond to our touch more easily than others. Certain notes seem to sound forth as the current of circumstances sweeps over the strings. And certain other notes are less easily vibrated. But we find that if we but make an effort of the will to restrain the utterance of some of these easily sounded strings, they will grow more difficult to sound, and less liable to be stirred by the passing breeze. And if we will pay attention to some of the other strings that have not been giving forth a clear tone, we will soon get them in good working order; their notes will chime forth clear and vibrant, and will drown the less pleasant sounds.

We have millions of unused brain-cells awaiting our cultivation. We are using but a few of them, and some of these we are working to death. We are able to give some of these cells a rest, by using other cells. The brain may be trained and cultivated in a manner incredible to one who has not looked into the subject. Mental attitudes may be acquired and cultivated, changed and discarded, at will. There is no longer any excuse for people manifesting unpleasant and harmful mental states.

We have the remedy in our own hands.

We acquire habits of thought, feeling, and action, by repeated use. We may be bom with a tendency in a certain direction, or we may acquire tendencies by suggestions from others; such as the examples of those around us, suggestions from reading, listening to teachers. We are a bundle of mental habits. Each time we indulge in an undesirable thought or habit, the easier does it become to repeat that thought or action. And the oftener we give forth a certain desirable thought, or perform a desirable action, the easier does it become for us to repeat that thought or action.

Mental scientists are in the habit of speaking of desirable thoughts or mental attitudes as 'positive,' and of the undesirable ones as 'negative.' There is a good reason for this. The mind instinctively recognizes certain things as good for the individual to which it belongs, and it clears the path for such thoughts, and interposes the least resistance to them. They have a much greater effect than an undesirable thought possesses, and one positive thought will counteract a number of negative thoughts. The best way to overcome undesirable or negative thoughts and feelings is to cultivate the positive ones. The positive thought is the strongest plant, and will in time starve out the negative one by withdrawing from it the nourishment necessary for its existence.

Of course the negative thought will set up a vigorous resistance at first, for it is a fight for life with it. In the slang words of the time, it 'sees its finish' if the positive thought is allowed to grow and develop; and, consequently, it makes things unpleasant for the individual until he has started well into the work of starving it out. Brain cells do not like to be laid on the shelf any more than does any other form of living energy, and they rebel and stmggle until they become too weak to do so. The best way is to pay as little attention as possible to these weeds ofthe mind, but put in as much time as possible watering, caring for and attending to the new and beautiful plants in the garden of the mind.

For instance, if you are apt to hate people, you can best overcome the negative thought by cultivating Love in its place. Think Love, and act it out, as often as possible. Cultivate thoughts of kindness, and act as kindly as you can to everyone with whom you come in contact. You will have trouble at the start, but gradually Love will master Hat e, and the latter will begin to droop and wither. If you have a tendency toward the 'blues' cultivate a smile, and a cheerful view of things. Insist upon your mouth wearing up-turned corners, and make an effort of the will to look upon the bright side of things. The 'blue-devils' will set up a fight, of course, but pay no attention to them—just go on cultivating optimism and cheerfulness. Let 'Bright, Cheerful and Happy,' be your watchword, and try to live it out.

These recipes may seem very old and timeworn, but they are psychological truths and may be used by you to advantage. If you once comprehend the nature of the thing, the affirmations and auto-suggestions of the several schools may be understood and taken advantage of. You may make yourself energetic instead of slothful, active instead of lazy, by this method. It is all a matter of practice and steady work. New Thought people often have much to say about 'holding the thought;' and, indeed, it is necessary to 'hold the thought' in order to accomplish results. But something more is needed. You must 'act out' the thought until it becomes a fixed habit with you. Thoughts take form in action; and in turn actions influence thought. So by 'acting out' certain lines of thought, the actions react upon the mind, and increase the development of the part of the mind having close relation to the act. Each time the mind entertains a thought, the easier becomes the resulting action—and each time an act is performed, the easier becomes the corresponding thought. So you see the thing works both ways—action and reaction. If you feel cheerful and happy, it is very natural for you to laugh. And if you will laugh a little, you will begin to feel bright and cheerful. Do you see what I am trying to get at? Here it is, in a nutshell: If you wish to cultivate a certain habit of action, begin by cultivating the mental attitude corresponding to it. And as a means of cultivating that mental attitude, start in to 'act out,' or go through, the motions of the act corresponding to the thought. Now, see if you cannot apply this rule. Take up something that you really feel should be done, but which you do not feel like doing. Cultivate the thought leading up to it—say to yourself: 'I like to do so and so,' and then go through the motions (cheerfully, remember!) and act out the thought that you like to do the thing. Take an interest in the doing—study out the best way to do it—put brains into it—take a pride in it—and you will find yourself doing the thing with a considerable amount of pleasure and interest—you will have cultivated a new habit.

If you prefer trying it on some mental trait of which you wish to be rid, it will work the same way. Start in to cultivate the opposite trait, and think it out and act it out for all you are worth.

Then watch the change that will come over you. Don't be discouraged at the resistance you will encounter at first, but sing gaily: 'I Can and I Will,' and get to work in earnest. The important thing in this work is to keep cheerful and interested. If you manage to do this, the rest will be easy.

CHAPTER 13

THE ATTRACTIVE POWER—DESIRE FORCE

Mental leaks—The man or woman in search of success—When Mental Force operates best—The Mind works on the sub-conscious plane along the line of the ruling passion or desire—Scattering thought-force—Getting out of the current of attraction—My personal experience—

'Love' at the bottom of the whole of life—The so-called 'chemical affinities '—Desire a manifestation of this Universal Life Love.

We have discussed the necessity of getting rid of fear, that your desire may have full strength with which to work. Supposing that you have mastered this part of the task, or at least started on the road to mastery, I will now call your attention to another important branch of the subject. I allude to the subject of mental leaks. No, I don't mean the leakage arising from your failure to keep your own secrets—that is also important, but forms another story. The leakage I am now referring to is that occasioned by the habit of having the attention attracted to and distracted by every passing fancy.

In order to attain a thing it is necessary that the mind should fall in love with it, and be conscious of its existence, almost to the exclusion of everything else. You must get in love with the thing you wish to attain, just as much as you would if you were to meet the girl or man you wished to marry. I do not mean that you should become a monomaniac upon the subject, and should lose all interest in everything else in the world—that won't do, for the mind must have recreation and change. But, I do mean that you must be so 'set' upon the desired thing that all else will seem of secondary importance. A man in love may be pleasant to everyone else, and may go through the duties and pleasures of life with good spirit, but underneath it all he is humming tb himself 'Just One Girl;' and every one of his actions is bent toward getting that girl, and making a comfortable home for her. Do you see what I mean? You must get in love with the thing you want, and you must get in love with it in earnest—none of this latter-day flirting, 'on-today and off-tomorrow' sort of love, but the good old-fashioned kind, that used to make it impossible for a young man to get to sleep unless he took a walk around his best girl's house, just to be sure it was still there.

That's the real kind! And the man or woman in search of success must make of that desired thing his ruling passion—he must keep his mind on the main chance. Success is jealous—that's why we speak of her as feminine. She demands a man's whole affection, and if he begins flirting with other fair charmers, she soon turns her back upon him. If a man allows his strong interest in the main chance to be sidetracked, he will be the loser. Mental Force operates best when it is concentrated. You must give to the desired thing your best and most earnest thought. Just as the man who is thoroughly in love will think out plans and schemes whereby he may please the fair one, so will the man who is in love with his work or business give it his best thought, and the result will be that a hundred and one plans will come into his field of consciousness, many of which are very important. The mind works on the subconscious plane, remember, and almost always along the lines of the ruling passion or desire. It will fix up things, and patch together plans and schemes, and when you need them the most it will pop them into your consciousness;, and you will feel like hurrahing, just as if you had received some valuable aid from outside.

But if you scatter your thought-force, the subconscious mind will not know just how to please you, and the result is that you are apt to be put off from this source of aid and assistance. Beside this, you will miss the powerful result of concentrated thought in the conscious working out of the details of your plans. And then again the man whose mind is full of a dozen interests fails to exert the attracting power that is manifested by the man of the one ruling passion, and he fails to draw to him persons, things, and results that will aid in the working out of his plans, and will also fail to place himself in the current of attraction whereby he is brought into contact with those who will be glad to help him because of harmonious interests.

I have noticed, in my own affairs, that when I would allow myself to be side-tracked by anything outside of my regular line of work, it would be only a short time before my receipts dropped off, and my business showed signs of a lack of vitality. Now, many may say that this was because I left undone some things that I would have done if my mind had been centered on the business. This is true; but I have noticed like results in cases where there was nothing to be done—cases in which the seed was sown, and the crop was awaited. And, in just such cases, as soon as I directed my thought to the matter the seed began to sprout. I do not mean that I had to send out great mental waves with the idea of affecting people—not a bit of it. I simply began to realize what a good thing I had, and how much people wanted it, and how glad they would be to know of it, and all that sort of thing, and lo! my thought seemed to vitalize the work, and the seed began to sprout. This is no mere fancy, for I have experienced it on several occasions; I have spoken to many others on the subject, and I find that our experiences tally perfectly. So don't get into the habit of permitting these mental leaks. Keep your Desire fresh and active, and let it get in its work without interference from conflicting desires. Keep in love with the thing you wish to attain—feed your fancy with it—see it as accomplished already, but don't lose your interest.Keep your eye on the main chance, and keep your one ruling passion strong and vigorous. Don't be a mental polygamist—one mental love is all that a man needs—that is, one at a time.

Some scientists have claimed that something that might as well be called 'Love' is at the bottom of the whole of life. They claim that the love of the plant for water causes it to send forth its roots until the loved thing is found. They say that the love of the flower for the sun, causes it to grow away from the dark places, so that it may receive the light. The so-called 'chemical affinities' are really a form of love. And Desire is a manifestation of this Universal Life Love. So I am not using a mere figure of speech when I tell you that you must love the thing you wish to attain. Nothing but intense love will enable you to surmount the many obstacles placed in your path. Nothing but that love will enable you to bear the burdens of the task. The more Desire you have for a thing, the more you Love it; and the more you Love it, the greater will be the attractive force exerted toward its attainment—both within yourself, and outside of you.

So love but one thing at a time—don't be a mental Mormon.

CHAPTER 14

THE GREAT DYNAMIC FORCES

The difference between the successful strong men and the unsuccessful weak men—Energy and Invincible Determination—Energy not rare—Wasted nerve-force—The Human Will—A great dynamic force—The people who have 'arrived'—Are they 'ordinary, 'after all?—Made of the stuff of those about them—Wherein does their greatness lie?—Belief in themselves—The right use of material—The 'trick' of greatness—The good things locked up in your mind—The inexhaustible supply.

You have noticed the difference between the successful and strong men in any walk of life, and the unsuccessful weak men around them. You are conscious of the widely differing characteristics of the two classes, but somehow find it difficult to express just in what the difference lies. Let us take a look at the matter.

Buxton said: 'The longer I live, the more certain I am that the great difference between men, the feeble and the powerful, the great and the insignificant, is energy and invincible determination—a purpose once fixed and then Death or Victory. That quality will do anything that can be done in this world—and no talents, no circumstances, no opportunities will make a two-legged creature a man without it.' I do not see how the idea could be more clearly expressed than Buxton has spoken. He has put his finger right in the center of the subject—his eye has seen into the heart of it.

Energy and invincible determination—these two things will sweep away mighty barriers, and will surmount the greatest obstacles. And yet they must be used together. Energy without determination will go to waste. Lots of men have plenty of energy—they are full to overflowing with it; and yet they lack concentration—they lack the concentrated force that enables them to bring their power to bear upon the right spot. Energy is not nearly so rare a thing as many imagine it to be. I can look around me at any time, and pick out a number of people I know who are full of energy—many of them are energy plus—and yet, somehow, they do not seem to make any headway.

They are wasting their energy all the time. Now they are fooling with this thing—now meddling with that. They will take up some trifling thing of no real interest or importance, and waste enough energy and nervous force to carry them through a hard day's work; and yet when they are through, nothing has been accomplished.

Others who have plenty of energy, fail to direct it by the power of the Will toward the desired end. 'Invincible determination'—those are the words. Do they not thrill you with their power? If you have something to do, get to work and do it. Marshal your energy, and then guide and direct it by your Will—bestow upon it that 'invincible determination' and you will do the thing. Everyone has within him a giant will, but the majority of us are too lazy to use it. We cannot get ourselves nerved up to the point at which we can say, truthfully: 'I Will.' If we can but screw up our courage to that point, and will then pin it in place so that it will not slip back, we will be able to call into play that wonderful power—the Human Will. Man, as a rule, has but the faintest conception of the power of the Will, but those who have studied along the occult teachings, know that the Will is one of the great dynamic forces of the universe, and if harnessed and directed properly it is capable of accomplishing almost miraculous things.

'Energy and Invincible Determination'—aren't they magnificent words? Commit them to memory—press them like a die into the wax of your mind, and they will be a constant inspiration to you in hours of need. If you can get these words to vibrating in your being, you will be a giant among pygmies. Say these words over and over again, and see how you are filled with new life—see how your blood will circulate—how your nerves will tingle. Make these words a part of yourself, and then go forth anew to the battle of life, encouraged and strengthened. Put them into practice. 'Energy and Invincible Determination'—let that be your motto in your work-a-day life, and you will be one of those rare men who are able to 'do things.' Many persons are deterred from doing their best by the fact that they underrate themselves by comparison with the successful ones of life, or rather, overrate the successful ones by comparison with themselves.

One of the curious things noticed by those who are brought in contact with the people who have 'arrived' is the fact that these successful people are not extraordinary after all. You meet with some great writer, and you are disappointed to find him very ordinary indeed. He does not converse brilliantly, and, in fact, you know a score of everyday people who seem far more brilliant than this man who dazzles you by his brightness in his books. You meet some great statesman, and he does not seem nearly so wise as lots of old fellows in your own village, who waste their wisdom upon the desert air. You meet some great captain of industry, and he does not give you the impression of the shrewdness so marked in some little bargain-driving trader in your own town. How is this, anyway? Are the reputations of these people fictitious, or what is the trouble? The trouble is this: You have imagined these people to be made of superior metal, and are disappointed to find them made of the same stuff as yourself and those about you. But, you ask, wherein does their greatness of achievement lie? Chiefly in this: Belief in themselves and in their inherent power, in their faculty to concentrate on the work in hand, when they are working, and in their ability to prevent leaks of power when they are not working. They believe in themselves, and make every effort count. Your village wiseman spills his wisdom on every comer, and talks to a lot of fools; when if he really were wise he would save up his wisdom and place it where it would do some work. The brilliant writer does not waste his wit upon every comer; in fact, he shuts the drawer in which he contains his wit, and opens it only when he is ready to concentrate and get down to business. The captain of industry has no desire to impress you with his shrewdness and 'smartness.' He never did, even when he was young. While his companions were talking and boasting, and 'blowing,' this future successful financier was 'sawin' wood and sayin' nuthin'.' The great people of the world—that is, those who have 'arrived'—are not very different from you, or me, or the rest of us—all of us are about the same at the base. You have only to meet them to see how very 'ordinary' they are, after all. But, don't forget the fact that they know how to use the material that is in them; while the rest of the crowd does not, and, in fact, even doubts whether the true stuff is there. The man or woman who 'gets there,' usually starts out by realizing that he or she is not so very different, after all, from the successful people that they hear so much about. This gives them confidence, and the result is they find out that they are able to 'do things.' Then they learn to keep their mouths closed, and to avoid wasting and dissipating their energy. They store up energy, and concentrate it upon the task at hand; while their companions are scattering their energies in every direction, trying to show off and let people know how smart they are. The man or woman who 'gets there,' prefers to wait for the applause that follows deeds accomplished, and cares very little for the praise that attends promises of what we expect to do 'some day,' or an exhibition of 'smartness' without works.

One of the reasons that people who are thrown in with successful men often manifest success themselves, is that they are able to watch the successful man and sort of 'catch the trick' of his greatness. They see that he is an everyday sort of man, but that he thoroughly believes in himself, and also that he does not waste energy, but reserves all his force for the actual tasks before him. And, profiting by example, they start to work and put the lesson into practice in their own lives.

Now what is the moral of this talk? Simply this: Don't undervalue yourself, or overvalue others.

Realize that you are made of good stuff, and that locked within your mind are many good things. Then get to work and unfold those good things, and make something out of that good stuff. Do this by attention to the things before you, and by giving to each the best that is in you, knowing that plenty of more good things are in you, ready for the fresh tasks that will come. Put the best of yourself into the undertaking on hand, and do not cheat the present task in favor of some future one. Your supply is inexhaustible. And don't waste your good stuff on the crowd of gapers, watchers and critics who are standing around watching you work. Save your good stuff for your job, and don't be in too much of a hurry for applause. Save up your good thoughts for 'copy' if you are a writer; save up your bright schemes for actual practice, if you are a business man; save up your wisdom for occasion, if you are a statesman; and, in each case, avoid the desire to scatter your pearls before—well, before the gaping crowd that wants to be entertained by a 'free show.' Nothing very 'high' about this teaching, perhaps, but it is what many of you need very much. Stop fooling, and get down to business. Stop wasting good raw material, and start to work making something worth while.

CHAPTER 15

CLAIMING YOUR OWN

Nothing too good for you—Your direct inheritance—Great things lost for want of asking—The Law takes you in earnest—You are a manifestation of the Whole Thing—You must first awaken to a realization that you are merely asking for 'your own '—The Law will do its work—The hypnotism of 'humility'—The great things in the Cosmos which await your coming of age—The playthings of life—Our game-tasks—The difference between the Master of Circumstances and the Slave of Circumstances.

In a recent conversation, I was telling a woman to pluck up courage and to reach out for a certain good thing for which she had been longing for many years, and which, at last, appeared to be in sight. I told her that it looked as if her desire was about to be gratified—that the Law of Attraction was bringing it to her. She lacked faith, and kept on repeating, 'Oh! it's too good to be true—it's too good for me!' She had not emerged from the worm-of-the-dust stage, and although she was in sight of the Promised Land she refused to enter it because it 'was too good for her.' I think I succeeded in putting sufficient 'ginger' into her to enable her to claim her own, for the last reports indicate that she is taking possession.

But that is not what I wish to tell you. I want to call your attention to the fact that nothing is too good for you—no matter how great the thing may be—no matter how undeserving you may seem to be. You are entitled to the best there is, for it is your direct inheritance. So don't be afraid to ask—demand—and take. The good things of the world are not the portion of any favored sons. They belong to all, but they come only to those who are wise enough to recognize that the good things are theirs by right, and who are sufficiently courageous to reach out for them. Many good things are lost for want of the asking. Many splendid things are lost to you because of your feeling that you are unworthy of them. Many great things are lost to you because you lack the confidence and courage to demand and take possession of them.

'None but the brave deserves the fair,' says the old adage, and the rule is true in all lines of human effort. If you keep on repeating that you are unworthy of the good thing—that it is too good for you—the Law will be apt to take you at your word and believe what you say. That's a peculiar thing about the Law—it believes what you say—it takes you in earnest. So beware what you say to it, for it will be apt to give credence. Say to it that you are worthy of the best there is, and that there is nothing too good for you. and you will be likely to have the Law take you in earnest, and say, 'I guess he is right; I'm going to give him the whole bakeshop if he wants it—he knows his rights, and what's the use of trying to deny it to him?' But if you say, 'Oh, it's too good for me!' the Law will probably say, 'Well, I wouldn't wonder but what that is so. Surely he ought to know, and it isn't for me to contradict him.' And so it goes.

Why should anything be too good for you? Did you ever stop to think just what you are? You are a manifestation of the Whole Thing, and have a perfect right to all there is. Or, if you prefer it this way, you are a child of the Infinite, and are heir to it all. You are telling the truth in either statement, or both. At any rate, no matter for what you ask, you are merely demanding your own. And the more in earnest you are about demanding it—the more confident you are of receiving it—the more will you use in reaching out for it—the surer you will be to obtain it.

Strong desire—confident expectation—courage in action—these things bring to you your own. But before you put these forces into effect, you must awaken to a realization that you are merely asking for your own, and not for something to which you have no right or claim. So long as there exists in your mind the last sneaking bit of doubt as to your right to the things you want, you will be setting up a resistance to the operation of the Law. You may demand as vigorously as you please, but you will lack the courage to act, if you have a lingering doubt of your right to the thing you want. If you persist in regarding the desired thing as if it belonged to another, instead of to yourself, you will be placing yourself in the position of the covetous or envious man, or even in the position of a tempted thief. In such a case your mind will revolt at proceeding with the work, for it instinctively will recoil from the idea of taking what is not your own—the mind is honest. But when you realize that the best the Universe holds belongs to you as a Divine Heir, and that there is enough for all without your robbing anyone else; then the friction is removed, and the barrier broken down, and the Law proceeds to do its work.

I do not believe in this 'humble' business. This meek and lowly attitude does not appeal to me—there is no sense in it, at all. The idea of making a virtue of such things, when Man is the heir of the Universe, and is entitled to whatever he needs for his growth, happiness and satisfaction! I do not mean that one should assume a blustering and domineering attitude of mind—that is also absurd, for true strength does not so exhibit itself. The blusterer is ' a self-confessed weakling—he blusters to disguise his weakness. The truly strong man is calm, self-contained, and carries with him a consciousness of strength which renders unnecessary the bluster and fuss of assumed strength. But get away from this hypnotism of 'humility'—this 'meek and lowly' attitude of mind. Remember the horrible example of Uriah Heep, and beware of imitating him. Throw back your head, and look the world square in the face. There's nothing to be afraid of—the world is apt to be as much afraid of you, as you are of it, anyway. Be a man, or woman, and not a crawling thing. And this applies to your mental attitude, as well as to your outward demeanor. Stop this crawling in your mind. See yourself as standing erect and facing life without fear, and you will gradually grow into your ideal.

There is nothing that is too good for you—not a thing. The best there is, is not beginning to be good enough for you; for there are still better things ahead. The best gift that the world has to offer is a mere bauble compared to the great things in the Cosmos that await your coming of age. So don't be afraid to reach out for these playthings of life—these baubles of this plane of consciousness. Reach out for them—grab a whole fistful—play with them until you are tired; that's what they are made for, anyway. They are made for our express use—not to look at, but to be played with, if you desire. Help yourself there's a whole shopful of these toys awaiting your desire, demand and taking. Don't be bashful! Don't let me hear any more of this silly talk about things being too good for you. Pshaw! You have been like the Emperor's little son thinking that the tin soldiers and toy drum were far too good for him, and refusing to reach out for them. But you don't find this trouble with children as a rule. They instinctively recognize that nothing is too good for them. They want all that is in sight to play with, and they seem to feel that the things are theirs by right. And that is the condition of mind that we seekers after the Divine Adventure must cultivate. Unless we become as little children we cannot enter the Kingdom of Heaven.

The things we see around us are the playthings of the Kindergarten of God, playthings which we use in our game-tasks. Help yourself to them—ask for them without bashfulness—demand as many as you can make use of—they are yours. And if you don't see just what you want, ask for it—there's a big reserve stock on the shelves, and in the closets. Play, play, play, to your heart's content. Learn to weave mats—to build houses with the blocks—to stitch outlines on the squares—play the game through, and play it well. And demand all the proper materials for the play—don't be bashful—there's enough to go round.

But-remember this! While all this be true, the best things are still only game-things—toys, blocks, mats, cubes, and all the rest. Useful, most useful for the learning of the lessons—pleasant, most pleasant with which to play—and desirable, most desirable, for these purposes. Get all the fun and profit out of the use of things that is possible. Throw yourself heartily into the game, and play it out—it is Good. But, here's the thing to remember—never lose sight of the fact that these good things are but playthings—part of the game—and you must be perfectly willing to lay them aside when the time comes to pass into the next class, and not cry and mourn because you must leave your playthings behind you. Do not allow yourself to become unduly attached to them—they are for your use and pleasure, but are not a part of you—not essential to your happiness in the next stage. Despise them not because of their lack of Reality—they are great things relatively, and you may as well have all the fun out of them that you can—don't be a spiritual prig, standing aside and refusing to join in the game. But do not tie yourself to them—they are good to use and play with, but not good enough to use you and to make you a plaything. Don't let the toys turn the tables on you.

This is the difference between the Master of Circumstances and the Slave of Circumstances. The Slave thinks that these playthings are real, and that he is not good enough to have them. He gets only a few toys, because he is afraid to ask for more, and he misses most of the fun. And then, considering the toys to be real, and not realizing that there are plenty more where these came from, he attaches himself to the little trinkets that have come his way, and allows himself to be made a slave of them. He is afraid that they may be taken away from him, and he is afraid to toddle across the floor and help himself to the others. The Master knows that all are his for the asking. He demands that which he needs from day to day, and does not worry about overloading himself; for he knows that there are 'lots more,' and that he cannot be cheated out of them. He plays, and plays well, and has a good time in the play—and he learns his Kindergarten lessons in the playing. But he does not become too much attached to his toys. He is willing to fling away the worn-out one, and reach out for a new one. And when he is called into the next room for promotion, he drops on the floor the worn-out toys of the day, and with glistening eyes and confident attitude of mind, marches into the next room—into the Great Unknown—with a smile on his face. He is not afraid, for he hears the voice of the Teacher, and knows that she is there waiting for him—in that Great Next Room.

CHAPTER 16

LAW, NOT CHANCE

The Attractive Power of Thought —'A matter of luck'—A magnificent illustration of the Law of Attraction—A strong belief as efficacious as a strong wish—The man who 'gets there '—The man who fails—No such thing as Chance—Law everywhere—Plan and purpose; cause and effect—The right vibrations—Getting into the current.

Some time ago I was talking to a man about the Attractive Power of Thought. He said that he did not believe that Thought could attract anything to him, and that it was all a matter of luck. He had found, he said, that ill luck relentlessly pursued him, and that everything he touched went wrong. It always had, and always would, and he had grown to expect it. When he undertook a new thing he knew beforehand that it would go wrong and that no good would come of it. Oh, no! there wasn't anything in the theory of Attractive Thought, so far as he could see; it was all a matter of luck! This man failed to see that by his own confession he was giving a most convincing argument in favor of the Law of Attraction. He was testifying that he was always expecting things to go wrong, and that they always came about as he expected. He was a magnificent illustration of the Law of Attraction—but he didn't know it, and no argument seemed to make the matter clear to him. He was 'up against it,' and there was no way out of it—he always expected the ill luck, and every occurrence proved that he was right, and that the Mental Science position was all nonsense. There are many people who seem to think that the only way in which the Law of Attraction operates is when one wishes hard, strong and steady. They do not seem to realize that a strong belief is as efficacious as a strong wish. The successful man believes in himself and in his ultimate Success, and, paying no attention to little setbacks, stumbles, tumbles and slips, presses on eagerly to the goal, believing all the time that he will get there. His views and aims may alter as he progresses, and he may change his plans or have them changed for him, but all the time he knows in his heart that he will eventually 'get there.' He is not steadily wishing he may get there—he simply feels it and believes it, and thereby sets into operation the strongest forces known in the world of thought.

The man who just as steadily believes he is going to fail will invariably fail. How could he help it? There is no special miracle about it. Everything he does, thinks and says is tinctured with the thought of failure. Other people catch his spirit, and fail to trust him or his ability, which occurrences he in turn sets down as but other exhibitions of his ill luck, instead of ascribing them to his belief and expectation of failure. He is suggesting failure to himself all the time, and he invariably takes on the effect of the autosuggestion. Then, again, he by his negative thoughts shuts up that portion of his mind from which should come the ideas and plans conducive to success and which do come to the man who is expecting success because he believes in it. A state of discouragement is not the one in which bright ideas come to us. It is only when we are enthused and hopeful that our minds work out the bright ideas which we may turn to account.

Men instinctively feel the atmosphere of failure hovering around certain of their fellows, and on the other hand recognize something about others which leads them to say, when they hear of a temporary mishap befalling such a one; 'Oh, he'll come out all right somehow—you can't down him.' It is the atmosphere caused by the prevailing Mental Attitude. Clear up your Mental Atmosphere! There is no such thing as chance. Law maintains everywhere, and all that happens happens because of the operation of Law. You cannot name the simplest thing that ever occurred by chance—try it, and then run the thing down to a final analysis, and you will see it as the result of Law. It is as plain as mathematics. Plan and purpose; cause and effect. From the movements of worlds to the growth of the grain of mustard seed—all the result of Law. The fall of the stone down the mountain-side is not chance—forces which had been in operation for centuries caused it. And back of that cause were other causes, and so on until the Causeless Cause is reached.

And Life is not the result of chance—the Law is here, too. The Law is in full operation whether you know it or not—whether you believe in it or not. You may be the ignorant object upon which the Law operates, and bring yourself all sorts of trouble because of your ignorance of or opposition to the Law. Or you may fall in with the operations of the Law—get into its current, as it were—and Life will seem a far different thing to you. You cannot get outside of the Law, by refusing to have anything to do with it. You are at liberty to oppose it and produce all the friction you wish to—it doesn't hurt the Law, and you may keep it up until you learn your lesson.

The Law of Thought Attraction is one name for the Law, or rather for one manifestation of it. Again I say, your thoughts are real things. They go forth from you in all directions, combining with thoughts of like kind—opposing thoughts of a different character—forming combinations—going where they are attracted—flying away from thought centers opposing them. And your mind attracts the thoughts of others, which have been sent out by them consciously or unconsciously. But it attracts only those thoughts which are in harmony with its own. Like attracts like, and opposites repel opposites, in the world of thought.

If you set your mind to the keynote of courage, confidence, strength and success, you attract to yourself thoughts of like nature; people of like nature; things that fit in the mental tune. Your prevailing thought or mood determines that which is to be drawn toward you—picks out your mental bedfellow. You are today setting into motion thought currents which will in time attract toward you thoughts, people and conditions in harmony with the predominant note of your thought. Your thought will mingle with that of others of like nature and mind, and you will be attracted toward each other, and will surely come together with a common purpose sooner or later, unless one or the other of you should change the current of his thoughts.

Fall in with the operations of the Law. Make it a part of yourself. Get into its currents. Maintain your poise. Set your mind to the keynote of Courage, Confidence and Success. Get in touch with all the thoughts of that kind that are emanating every hour from hundreds of minds. Get the best that is to be had in the thought world. The best is there, so be satisfied with nothing less. Get into partnership with good minds. Get into the right vibrations. You must be tired of being tossed about by the operations of the Law—get into harmony with it.

PART – II

PRACTICAL MENTAL INFLUENCE

CHAPTER 1

THE LAW OF VIBRATION

Students of history find a continuous chain of reference to the mysterious influence of one human mind over that of others. In the earliest records, traditions and legends may be found giving reference to the general belief that it was possible for an individual to exert some weird uncanny power over the minds of other persons, which would influence the latter for good or evil. And more than this, the student will find an accompanying belief that certain individuals are possessed of some mental power which bends even 'things' and circumstances to its might.

Away back in the dim past of man's history on this planet, this belief existed, and it has steadily persisted in spite of the strenuous opposition of material science, even unto the present day. The years have not affected the belief, and in these dawning days of the Twentieth Century it has taken on a new strength and vitality, for its adherents have boldly stepped to the front, and confronting the doubting materialistic thinkers, have claimed the name of 'Science' for this truth and have insisted that it be taken, once and for all, from the category of superstition, credulity and ignorant phantasm.

Were it not pitiable, it would be amusing to glance at the presumptuous, complacent, smug, self—satisfied position of the materialistic school of thinkers, who would brush aside as a foolish delusion that which many of the wisest men of a past age have accepted and taught as the truth. The modem 'know—it—alls' would sneer contemptuously at facts that are known to be of actual occurrence in the daily lives of thousands of intelligent people, and which the experience of humankind has demonstrated for many centuries, in all lands and all races.

The Whole trouble lies in the dogmatic assumption of the materialistic school that what is known as 'mind' is merely some peculiar action of the material brain, some writers even holding that 'the brain secretes thought, just as the liver secretes bile.' They refuse to see that the operation of Mind is a manifestation of energy known as electricity, magnetism, light, heat, gravitation, cohesion, etc. Because mental energy does not register the vibrations of these lower forms of energy, they conclude that the higher mental energy does not exist. Having formulated a theory to suit their materialistic conceptions, they try to ignore all facts not consistent with their theory.

If they find a fact that will not squeeze into their narrow theory well, 'so much the worse for the fact,' as a writer has said and they promptly ignore or dispute it.

As a matter of truth, the investigator is not compelled to resort to metaphysical explanations to account for the phenomena of Mental Influence. The very facts of physical science itself, if rightly interpreted, will give the clue to the mystery; and will point the steps of the honest investigator toward the path where he may find the solution of the perplexing riddle. Although we know that the real solution lies in the metaphysical realm, still even physical science will corroborate the facts of its metaphysical sister science, and instead of contradicting the latter will actually go far toward furnishing analogous facts and principles basis for a theory of metaphysical facts.

The student will see at once that so far as physical science is concerned, it must begin at the phenomenon of 'Thought Transference,' for in that phase of the subject may be found an elementary principle in evidence in many other forms of phenomena. We have given many instances of 'Thought Transference' in the two proceeding volumes of this series, entitled 'Mind Reading' and 'Psychomancy,' respectively, and so we need not repeat the same in this place. The main fact is that 'Thought Transference' does exist, and may be accounted for upon purely scientific grounds, without calling in the truths of metaphysical thought. We know that this is a strong statement, and a positive assertion, but we also know that the same may be demonstrated. Let us consider this phase of the subject.

In the first place, physical science teaches that underlying all forms, degrees and apparent differences in matter and energy, there is to be found a manifestation of some elementary energy, which manifests in what is known as 'Vibrations.' Everything in the material world is in vibration—ever manifesting a high degree of motion. Without vibration there would be no such thing as a material universe. From the electronic—corpuscles which science teaches compose the atom; up through the atom and molecule, until the most complex forms of matter are manifested, there is the ever—present Vibration. And through all forms of energy, light, heat, electricity, magnetism and the rest, Vibration is also ever present. In fact, physical science itself teaches that not only is Vibration the basic force underlying other forces and the various forms of matter, but also that the apparent differences between the various forms of matter, and also between the various forms of energy, are caused simply and solely by the varying degrees of Vibration manifested.

Just as the difference between the lowest tone that can be distinguished by the ear of man, and the highest note that can be distinguished by the same organ of sense, is merely a difference between the rate of Vibration—just as is the difference between the dull red color at one end of the spectrum, and the violet at the other end, with the intervening colors known as indigo, blue green, yellow and orange, with all the combinations of shades arising from them—just as the difference between the greatest degree of cold known to Science, and the greatest degree of heat that can be conceived of—just as these great differences due solely and wholly to varying rates of Vibration—so is the difference between and all forms of matter or force simply a matter of the rate of Vibration. In short, all material and physical 'Things' are simply manifestations of some 'infinite and eternal energy from which all things proceed,' their differences resulting merely from the different degree of Vibration being manifested in them. Remember, that this is not 'vague philosophy' or 'airy metaphysics' or 'spiritualistic vagaries' (to quote from the materialistic writers), but facts claimed and admitted by the greatest physical scientists of the age, as a reference to their lectures and textbooks will prove to anyone.

And, more than this, any intelligent physical scientist will tell you that Science has every reason to believe that there are great fields of energy and force, the Vibrations of which are far too high for even the delicate instruments of science to record, but which nevertheless exist and manifest effects. It was only the other day that Science was able to 'catch' the 'X—rays' and other forms of high Radio—activity, and yet these rays and forces had always existed. And tomorrow Science will perfect instruments capable of registering still higher forms of energy. And bye—and—bye, some scientist will perfect an instrument capable of registering and recording the subtle vibrations of Thought, and perhaps in time someone will perfect that instrument so that it will not only record such Thought vibrations and waves, but, like the phonograph, it will be able to reproduce and send forth similar vibrations so that others may feel the thoughts, just as they now hear the sounds from the phonograph. Such a prediction is no more wonderful then would have been the prediction of the telephone, the phonograph, the wireless telegraph and suridry other discoveries and inventions a hundred years ago.

Did you ever think that there are colors that the eye cannot see, but which delicate instruments clearly register? In fact, the rays of tight which sunburn the face, and which register on the photographic plate are not visible to the eye. The eye sees the lower rays, but only instruments adapted for the purpose detect the higher ones. Your eye cannot see the X—ray as it passes through the room, but the plate will catch it, and its light may make a photograph. The rays of light visible to the eyes are only the lower ones—the higher ones are far beyond the power of the eye to record, and beyond even the range of the most delicate instrument there exist rays and waves of light of such high vibratory rate as to defy even its power to record.

Did you ever know that there are sounds unheard by human ears that the microphone will catch and magnify? Scientific imagination dreams of instruments that will catch the songs of the mite—like insects, and magnify them until they can be distinguished. There are waves of electricity that may pass through your body, unperceived by you, and yet powerful enough to run light electric lights. Listen to the words of certain eminent scientists.

Prof. Elisha Gary, a celebrated scientist and teacher, has said: 'There is much food for speculation in the thought that there exists sound waves that no human ear can hear, and color waves of light that no eye can see. The long, dark, soundless space between 40, 000 and 400,000,000,000,000 vibrations per second, and the infinity of range beyond 700,000,000,—000,000 vibrations per second, where light ceases, in the universe of motion, makes it possible to indulge in speculation.'

Prof. Williams, the well—known scientific writer, has said: 'There is no gradation between the most rapid undulations or trembling that produces our sensations of sound, and the slowest of those which give rise to our sensations of gentlest warmth. There is a huge gap between them, wide enough to include another world of motion, all lying between our world of sound and our world of heat and light; and there is no good reason whatever for supposing that matter is incapable of such intermediate activity, or that such activity may not give rise to intermediate sensations, provided that there are organs for taking up and sensitizing their movements.'

And, so you see that in the scientific theory of Vibrations, there may be found plenty of room for a scientific explanation of all that is claimed by adherents of the truth of Mental Influence, without getting out of the region of physical science, and without invading the plane of metaphysics. And there are many more proofs from the same source, which we may touch upon as we proceed.

There is but one Truth, and it manifests on all planes—the Spiritual; the Mental; and the Physical—and manifestations agree and coincide. So no Mentalist need fear the test of Physical Science, for each plane will bear out the facts and phenomena of the ones below or above it—the Three are but varying phases of One. In this little work we shall hug close to the plane of Physical Science, because by so doing we will be able to make the subject much clearer to many than if we had attempted to express the teaching in Metaphysical terms. There is no contradiction in the end. Each bit of Truth must dovetail into every other bit, for all are parts of the Whole.

CHAPTER 2

THOUGHT WAVES

In our last chapter we have seen that Vibration was to be found underlying all manifestations of energy, and all forms of matter. We also quoted two distinguished scientists whose words showed that there were fields of vibratory energy not filled by any known forms of energy, the inference being that inasmuch as there are no gaps in nature's processes these unknown fields must be occupied by certain forms of energy not known as yet to physical science. The teachings of the occultists of all lands and ages, as also those of modem Mental Science, are to the effect that the Mind, in its manifestation of Thought in the brain, generates a form of energy of intensely high Vibration, which energy may be, and is, projected in vibratory waves from the brains of other persons within its field of influence.

All students of Mental Influence have noticed the close resemblance that is manifested between the phenomena of electrical and magnetic energy on the one hand and the phenomena of mental energy on the other. So close is the analogy that one may take the proven facts of science relating to electrical and magnetic phenomena and confidently proceed with the certainty of finding a strikingly close correspondence in the field of mental phenomena. And the recognition of this fact is helping the workers in the mental field group together the varied phenomena that come under their notice, and to work out the theory and practice of Mental Influence.

In the first place, it is now a fact well known and accepted by investigators that the generation of Thought and the manifestation of Mental States occasions a 'burning up' of brain matter, and the consequent production of a form of energy of high vibratory power. Physiologists recognize this fact, and the textbooks make reference to it. Experiments have shown that the temperature of the brain is increased in accordance with the intensity of Feeling and Thought, and that there is undoubtedly a generation of energy and a consumption of brain matter which bears a very close resemblance to the process of the generation of electrical energy. And this being conceded, it follows that this energy once released must be emanated or sent forth from the brain in the manner akin to the emanation of other known forms of energy, i.e., in the form of 'waves' of vibratory force. Light and Heat travel in this way—so do electricity and magnetism—so do the forces of Radio—activity. And the investigators of Mental Influence have demonstrated by their experiments that there is such a thing as Thought—induction, and many other phases of manifestation similar to that exhibited by electricity and magnetism.

Flammarion, the well—known and eminent French scientist, has said on the subject. 'We sum up, therefore, our preceding observations by the conclusion that one mind can act at a distance upon another, without the habitual medium of words, or any other visible means of communication. It appears to us altogether unreasonable to reject this conclusion if we accept the facts. The conclusion will be abundantly demonstrated. There is nothing unscientific, nothing romantic in admitting that an idea can influence a brain from a distance. The action of one human being upon another, from a distance, is a scientific fact, it is as certain as the existence of Paris, of Napoleon, of Oxygen, or of Sirius.' The same authority also states: 'There can be no doubt that our physical force creates a movement in the either which transmits itself afar like all movements in the ether, becomes perceptible to brains in harmony with our own. The transformation of a psychic action into an ethereal movement, and the reverse, may be analogous to what takes place on a telephone, where the receptive plate, which is identical with the plate at the other end, reconstructs the sonorous movement transmitted, not by means of sound, but by electricity. But these are only comparisons.'

When a Thought or feeling is generated in the mind or brain of a person, the energy generated flows forth from the brain of the person in the form of waves of mental energy, spreading from the immediate neighborhood of the thinker to a distance proportioned to the strength of the thought or feeling. These Thought—Waves have the property of awakening similar vibrations in the minds of other persons coming within their field of force, according to the laws of Mental Influence, which law shall be explained in the next chapter.

As we proceed with our consideration of the subject of Mental Influence, in the succeeding chapters, we shall see the many and varied forms of manifestation of Thought—Waves. At this point we shall merely view the phenomena in a general way.

Thought—Waves are manifested in a variety of forms and phases. Some are the waves emanated from the minds of all thinkers, unconsciously and without purpose, and usually without much force. Others are sent forth with great force, and travel far, manifesting a degree of influence commensurate with the force with which they are projected. Others are directed purposely toward certain individuals or places, and travel along rapidly in a straight line to the point which they have been directed or aimed. Others are sent forth with great strength and power, but instead of being directed toward any particular person or place, are designed to sweep around in great whirlpools of energy affecting all who happen to fall within their field force.

You will readily understand that there is a great difference between Thought—Waves sent forth idly and unconsciously, and without knowledge of the underlying laws of Mental Influence, and those projected with a full knowledge of the laws governing the phenomena and urged on and directed by a powerful Will of the sender. The force is the same, but the degree of its power, and the measure of its effects are determined by the conditions of its sending force.

The vibratory force of these Thought—Waves does not cease with the sending forth of the wave, but persists for a long time afterward. Just as heat in a room persists long after the fire in the stove has been extinguished—just as the perfume of the flower exists in a room long after the flower has been removed—just as a ray of light travels through space for millions of miles, and for centuries after the star itself has been blotted out of existence—just as any and all forms of vibratory energy persist in manifesting after the initial impulse has been withdrawn—so do the vibrations of Thought continue long after the thought, yes, long after the brain which sent them forth has passed into dust.

There are many places today filled with the thought—vibrations of minds long since passed outside of the body. There are many places filled with the strong vibrations of tragedies long since enacted there. Every place has an atmosphere of its own, arising from the thought vibrations set in motion by the various persons who have inhabited or occupied them. Every city has its own mental atmosphere, which has an effect upon persons moving into them. Some are lively, some dull, some progressive, some old—fogeyish, some moral, some immoral—the result of the character of the early settlers and leading spirits of the places. The atmosphere affects persons moving into these towns, and either sinks to the general level, or else, if strong enough, help to change the mental tone of the place. Sometimes a change in conditions brings a large influx of new people to the town, and the mental waves of the newcomers tend to bring about a marked change in the local mental atmosphere. These facts have been noted by many observing people who were, perhaps, not familiar with the laws and principles underlying the phenomena.

Many have of course noticed the differing atmosphere of stores, offices and other places of business. Some of such places give one an air of confidence and trust; others create a feeling of suspicion and mistrust; some convey an impression of active, wide awake management, while others impress one as being behind the times and suffering from lack of alert, active management. Did you ever stop to think that these different atmospheres were caused by the prevailing mental attitudes of those in charge of the places? The managers of business places send forth Thought—Waves of their own, and their employees naturally falling into the pace set for them, sending forth similar vibrations, and before long the whole place is vibrating on a certain scale. Let a change in the management occur and see what a change soon manifests itself.

Did you ever notice the mental atmospheres of the houses you happened to visit? You may experience and recognize all of the varying notes in the mental scale of their occupants. From some thresholds harmony manifests itself, while others breathe in harmony as soon as you step over the threshold. Some radiate mental warmth, while others seem as cold as an iceberg. Think for a moment and recall the various houses or places you visit, and see how the mental vibrations of the inmates manifest themselves to a visitor.

The low quarters of our cities, the dens of vice and haunts of dissipation vibrate with the character of thought and feeling of those inhabiting them. And the weak—willed visitor is thus tempted. And, in the same way, certain places are filled with strong, helpful, elevating vibrations, which tend to lift up and elevate those coming within their circle of influence. Thoughts and Feelings are contagious, by reason of the Law of Vibration and Mental Induction. When this law is understood the individual is enabled to protect and improve himself. Such Knowledge brings Strength.

CHAPTER 3

MENTAL INDUCTION

As we stated in the preceding chapter, the phenomena of Mental Influence bears a striking analogy to that of the electrical or magnetic energy. Not only is this so in the phase of wave motion and transmission, but also in the phase of induction, as we shall see presently.

In physical science the term Induction is used to indicate that quality in a manifestation of energy which tends to reproduce in a second object the vibrations manifesting in the first object, without direct contact between the two bodies. A magnet will induce magnetism in another object removed from its space. An electrified object will tend to produce similar vibrations in another object by induction, over great spaces. Heat waves travel along the ether, and tend to produce heat vibrations in objects far removed, notably in the case of the sun and the earth. Even sound waves will affect other objects in this way, as in the well—known instance of the glass or vase 'singing' in response to the musical note sounded afar off. In fact, we see and hear by processes similar to those described.

And in this same manner that Thought—Waves carry the vibrations of the mind sending them forth to great distances, or lesser ones, tending to set up similar vibrations in the middle of other persons within their field force. Thus a person feeling a strong degree of anger will pour forth waves of that degree of mental vibration, which, coming in contact with the brains of other persons, tend to set up a similar feelings or emotions and thus cause the person to 'feel cross' or 'peevish' or even to manifest a similar angry state of mind. We all know how easily a fight is started by a very angry person in a room sending forth violent vibrations. One has but to remember the instances of mob violence to see how easily the 'contagion of hate and anger' spread among people who allow themselves to be influenced. And not only is this true of undesirable emotions and feelings, but also of desirable ones. The influence of a good man who happens to be strong mentally spreads among those around him, influencing in them for good.

Orators, actors, preachers and teachers send forth strong within toll currents, which tend to produce mental conditions on the part of their hearers corresponding to the feeling held by the mind of the speaker. When you remember how this speaker swayed your feelings, or how that actor made you weep with pity, shiver with fear, or laugh with joy, you will see how Mental induction acts.

But not only is this true when we are in the actual presence of the person sending out the Thought—Waves, but it is equally true that we are influenced by persons far removed from us in space, often without their knowledge or intent, although sometimes (in the case of one who understands the principal most) with full knowledge and intent.

The ether with which space is filled carries these Thought—Waves in all directions, and the surface of the earth, particularly in the densely occupied portions, is filled with these waves. These waves, carrying the mental vibrations, coming in contact with each other, tend to set up combinations on one hand, or else neutralize each other on the other hand. That is to say, if two sets of waves of a similar nature meet there is likely to be a combination formed between them just as between two chemicals having an affinity for each other. In this way the 'mental atmosphere' of places, towns, houses, etc., is formed. On the other hand if currents of opposing vibrations came in contact with each other, there will be manifested a conflict between the two, in which each will lose in proportion to its weakness, and the result will be either a neutralization of both or else a combination having vibrations of an average rate. For instance, if two currents of mental energy meet, one being a thought of Love and the other Hate, they will neutralize each other if they are equal, or if one is stronger than the other, it will persist but robbed of much of its strength. If it were not for this neutralizing effect we would be largely at the mercy of stray currents of thought. Nature protects us in this way, and also by rendering us immune to a considerable extent.

But nevertheless we are affected by these waves to a considerable extent, unless we have learned to throw them off by knowledge of the laws and an enforcement of them by practice. We all know how great waves of feeling spread over the town, city or country, sweeping people off their balance. Great waves of political enthusiasm, or War spirits, or prejudice for or against certain people, or groups of people, sweep over places and cause men to act in a manner that they will afterward regret when they come to themselves and consider their acts in cold blood. Demagogues will sway them or magnetic leaders who wish to gain their votes or patronage; and they will be led into acts of mob violence, or similar atrocities, by yielding to these waves of 'contagious' thought. On the other hand we all know how great waves of religious feeling sweep over a community upon the occasion of some great 'revival' excitement or fervor.

The effect of these Thought—Waves, so far as the power of induction is concerned, of course depends very materially upon the strength of the thought or feeling being manifested in the mind sending them forth. The majority of persons put but little force into the mental manifestations, but here and there is to be found a thinker whose Thought—Waves are practically 'a stream of living will' and which of course have a very strong inductive effect upon the minds of others with whom the waves come in contact. But it likewise follows that a number of persons thinking along the same lines will produce a great volume of power by a combination of their thought currents into great streams of mental force.

Then again there is another feature of the case that we must not lose sight of, and that is the Attraction between minds, by virtue of which one draws to himself the Thought—Waves of others whose thoughts are in accord with his own. The contrary is true, for there is Repulsion between the minds of persons and the Thought—Waves of others whose thoughts are not in accord with his own. The contrary is true, for there is Repulsions between the minds of persons and the Thought—Waves of others antagonistic to their thoughts. To quote a well—worn and much—used expression to illustrate this truth, 'Like attracts Like,' and 'Birds of a Feather flock together.' There is ever in operation this marvelous law of Attraction and Repulsion of Mental Energy—Persons allowing their thoughts to run along certain lines, and permitting the feelings to be expressed in certain ways, draw to themselves the Thought—Waves and mental influences of others keyed to the same mental key—note. And likewise they repel the waves and influences of an opposing nature. This is an important fact to remember in one's everyday life. Good attracts Good and repels Evil. Evil attracts Evil and repels Good. The predominant Mental Attitude serves to attract similar influences and to repel the opposing ones. Therefore watch carefully the character and nature of your thoughts—cultivate the desirable ones and repress the undesirable ones. Verily 'As a man thinketh in his heart, so is he.' Some Thought—Waves sent forth with but little strength travel slowly and do not proceed very far from their place of emanation, but creep along like some smoke or fog, lazily and yielding.

Other thoughts charged with a greater intensity of desire or will, dart forth vigorously like an electric spark, and often travel great distances. The weak Thought—Waves do not last a very long time, but fade away or become neutralized or dissipated by stronger, forces. But the strong thoughts persist for a long time, retaining much of their vitality and energy.

In the same manner the Thought—Waves of a person will continue to vibrate around him wherever he goes, and those coming in contact with him will be impressed by the character of his vibrations in this way. Some men send forth gloomyvibrations in this way. Some men send forth gloomy vibrations, which you feel when you come in contact with them. Others radiate good—cheer, courage and happiness, which conditions are induced in those with whom they come in contact. Many people will manifest these qualities so strongly that one can notice the effect the moment such persons enter a room. They carry their atmosphere with them, and the same is induced in the minds of others around them.

In the same way some people carry with them vibrations of Will—Power and Masterfulness that beat upon the minds of others, making them feel the power of such persons and conquering their own will—power and changing their desires. Others manifest a strong power of Fascination or Attraction, in a similar manner which tends to draw others to them and to their desires and wishes. Not only does this principle operate in the phase of general mental atmospheres, but also in the phase of direct personal influence.

All forms of Mental influence operate along the lines of Mental induction, as herein described. The principle is the same in all cases and instances, although the manner of operation varies according to the particular phase of the phenomena manifested. Remember this as we proceed, and you will be able to understand the subject much better.

CHAPTER 4

MENTAL CONCENTRATION

The two principal factors in the manifestation of Mental Influence, in all of its forms, are what are know as (1) Concentration, and (2) Mertal Imagining. The first of these factors shall be considered in this chapter, the succeeding chapter taking up the consideration of the second. 'Concentration' is a word derived from two Latin words, i.e., 'con,' a prefix meaning ' to;' and 'centrum,' meaning 'center' or 'fixed central point.' The two words combined mean, literally, 'to bring to a common point; to focus,' etc. Thus the word 'Concentration' is seen to mean, literally, 'the act or state of bringing to a fixed point or focus.

Borrowing an analogous illustration from physical science, we readily see that the highest forms of energy, force or power are manifested by bringing the force to a focus, center, or common point thereby directing to that point the entire energy employed, instead of allowing it to become dissipated over a larger area. The electricity generated by a battery or dynamo, if allowed to diffuse itself over a large surface manifests but a small degree of the power that may be obtained from it by compelling it to discharge itself from a small point of focus. The same is true regarding the power of steam, which manifests great power by being forced to discharge itself through a small point or opening instead of being permitted to spread itself widely in the air. The same law applies to gunpowder, which manifests force by its gases being compelled to escape through the small gun—barrel instead of spreading in all directions, which it would do if unconfined. Another familiar example is that of the sun glass, or 'burning—glass,' which brings the rays of the sun to a common point or focus, greatly intensifying the heat and light by reason thereof.

The occult masters have ever impressed upon their pupils the importance and necessity of acquiring the power of Mental Concentration, and all trained and developed occultists have practiced and persevered toward this end, the result being that some of them attained almost miraculous mental powers and influence. All occult phenomena are caused in this way, and all occult power depends upon it. Therefore the student of Mental Influence should devote much thought, time and practice to this most important branch of the subject.

It is a fact known to all students of mental phenomena that very few persons possess more than a very small degree of concentration. They allow their mental forces to become scattered and dissipated in all directions, and obtain little or no results from the same. In the degree that a man is able to concentrate, so is he able to manifests mental power. A man's power of mental concentration is to a great extent his measure of greatness.

Mental Concentration, in practice, consists of focusing the mind upon a given subject, or object, firmly and fixedly, and then holding it there for a certain time, fully intent upon its object, and not allowing itself to be diverted or attracted from its object. It likewise consists in the correlative power of then detaching the mind from that subject, or object, and either allowing it to rest, or else focusing it upon another object. In other words, it either gives undivided attention or else inhibits (or 'shuts off') attention from the given subject or object.

To the reader who has had no experience along the lines of Mental Concentration, it may seem like a very easy Mental Influence task to focus the mind upon a subject, and then hold it there firmly and fixedly. But a little practice will undeceive such a person and will bring him to a realizing sense of the difficulty of the task. The mind is a very restless thing, and its tendency is to dance from one thing to another, darting here and there, soon tiring of continued attention, and like a spoiled child, seeking a new object upon which to exercise itself .On the other hand, many people allow their minds to concentrate (involuntarily) upon whatever may strike their fancy, and, forgetting everything else, they give themselves up to the object attracting their attention for the moment, often neglecting duties and important interests, and becoming day dreamers instead of firm thinkers. This involuntary concentration is a thing to be avoided, for it is the allowing of the attention to escape the control of the will. The Mental Concentration of the occultists is a very different thing, and is solely in control of the will, being applied when desirable, and taken off or inhibited when undesirable.

The trained occultist will concentrate upon a subject or object with a wonderful intensity, seemingly completely absorbed in the subject or object before him, and oblivious to all else in the world. And yet, the task accomplished or the given time expired, he will detach his mind from the object and will be perfectly fresh, watchful and wide—awake to the next matter before him. There is a difference in being controlled by involuntary attention, which is a species of self—hypnotizing, and the control of the attention, which is an evidence of mastery.

The secret of Mental Concentration lies in the control of the Attention. And the control of the Attention lies in the exercise of the Will.

A celebrated French psychologist has well said: 'The authority is subject to the superior authority of the Ego. I yield it or I withhold it as I please. I direct it in turn to several points. I concentrate it upon each point as long as my will can stand the effort.' Sully says: 'Attention may be roughly defined as the active self—direction of the mind to any object which presents itself at the moment.' All of the occult authorities begin teaching their pupils Attention as the first step toward Mental Concentration. They instruct the pupil to examine some familiar object, and endeavor to see as many details as possible in the object. Then after hearing the pupil's report, the master sends him back to the task, bidding him seek for new details, and so on until at last the pupil has discovered about all concerning the object that can be discovered. The next day a new object is given to him, and the process is repeated. First simple objects are given, and then more complex ones, until at last objects of great complexity are easily mastered. In this way not only is the power of close observation highly developed, but also the faculty of Attention becomes so highly strengthened that the pupil is able to exert the greatest amount of Mental Concentration with scarcely the consciousness of effort. And such a person then becomes a very giant in the manifestation of Mental Influence. For he is able to mold his mind 'one—pointed,' as the Orientals describe it, until he has focused and directed a mighty degree of Mental Influence toward the desired object. Among the practices imposed upon their pupils by occult masters may be named Mathematics, Drawing, Analysis, etc. You will readily see why this is. To begin with, Mathematics requires the undivided attention of the student—unless he concentrates upon his examples, he will not be able to work out their solution. And, according to the principle in Nature that 'practice makes perfect,' and that 'exercise develops power,' the practice of the mind along lines requiring voluntary attention and mental concentration will inevitably result in the acquirement of the mental control and power, which renders possible the strongest manifestation of Mental Influence. The person who uses Mental Influence must certainly possess the power of focusing the force to a common point, in order to manifest the greatest amount of power and influence. And that faculty of focusing results from the training of the mind along the lines of Concentration. And Concentration arises from the mastery of Voluntary Attention. So there you have the whole matter in a nutshell. So your first step toward acquiring Mental Influence should be to cultivate Voluntary Attention.

We might fill page after page with exercises designed to strengthen your faculty of Voluntary Attention, but what would be the use? The best plan is to set you to work to find something upon which to concentrate, for the very search will develop attention. Look around you for some object to study in detail. Then concentrate your attention upon it until you have seen all there is about it to be seen, then take up another object and pursue the practice further. Take a page—this page, if you will, and count the number of words on it. Then see how many words are required to fill each line, on an average, then see how many letters there are in each word, in each line, on the whole page. Then go over the page and see if any words are misspelled, or if any of the letters are imperfect, etc. In short, get acquainted with this page, until you know all about it. Then take up another page, and after studying it in the same way, compare the two. And so on. Of course this will be very dry and tedious unless you take an interest in it. And, remembering just what the exercise is designed for may arouse this interest.

After practicing this way for a short time each day, you will begin to find that you are able to bestow greater attention upon objects upon which you are trying to manifest Mental Influence.

You are developing Concentration, and that is the great secret of the use of Mental Influence, and explains the difference in its manifestation among men. Think over this.

CHAPTER 5

MENTAL IMAGING

In our last chapter we called your attention to the first of the two principal factors in the manifestation of Mental Influence, namely, 'Mental Concentration.' In the present chapter we shall consider the second factor tending to render possible the said manifestation, namely, 'Mental Imaging.' What is known as a 'Mental Image, in occultism, is the mental creation, in the imagination of a 'picture' of the things, events or conditions that one desires to be manifested or, materialized in actual effect. A moments thought will show you that unless you know 'just what' you desire, you can take no steps toward attaining it on any plane of manifestation. And the more clearly your desires are perceived in your imagination, the clearer is the work of proceeding toward the realization of that desire. A Mental Image gives you a framework upon which to work. It is like the drawing of the architect, or the map of the explorer. Think over this for a few moments until you get the idea firmly fixed in your mind.

And now the same rule holds well on the plane in which the manifestation of Mental influence takes place. The occultist first builds up, in his imagination, a Mental Image or Picture of the conditions he wishes to bring about, and then by concentrating his influence strongly, instead of in a haphazard way as is the case with the majority of people who do not understand the laws and principles underlying the manifestations of the forces of mind. The Mental Image gives shape and direction to the forces, which is being concentrated upon the desired object or subject. It may be compared to the image on the glass of the Magic Lantern, through which the focused rays of the lamp pass, the result being that a corresponding image is reproduced upon the screen or curtain beyond. The analogy is a very close-one indeed, if we remember that the minds of the majority of people are more or less blank screens or curtains upon which play the pictures produced there by outside influences, suggestions, environments, etc., for very few people realize their individuality, and are merely reflections of the thoughts and ideas of other people.

An eminent authority, Sir Francis Galton, who was one of the leading authorities upon psychology of preceding generations, has said on this subject: 'The free action of a high visualizing faculty is of much importance in connection with the higher processes of generalized thought. A visual image is the most perfect form of mental representation whatever the shape, position and relations of objects to space are concerned I lie-best workmen are those who visualize the whole of what they propose to do before they take a tool in their hands. Strategists, artists of all denominations, physicists who contrive new experiments, and in short, all who do not follow routine, have a need for it. A faculty that is of importance in all technical and artistic occupations, that gives accuracy to our perceptions and justice to our generalizations, is starved by lazy disuse instead of being cultivated judiciously in such a way as will, on the whole, bring the best return. I believe that a serious study of the best way of developing and utilizing this faculty, without prejudice to the practice of abstract thought in symbols, is one of the many pressing desires in the yet unformed science of education.' And what Galton has said of the value of the use of this faculty of the mind in the affairs of the material plane, so it is likewise true of the manifestations on the mental plane. You know that the clearer a Mental Picture you possess of anything that you want—the better you know just what you want—and the better you know the latter, the better able you are to take steps to get it. Many people go through life wanting 'something,' but not really knowing 'just what' they do want. Is it any wonder .that they do not realize or materialize their desires any better? And the same thing holds well on the plane of manifestation of Mental Influence. If one wishes to materialize anything by the use of the influence, is he not handicapped by a lack of Mental Image of just what he wants to materialize, and is he not helped very much by the creation of a mental 'pattern' or plan, in the shape of a mental picture, through and around which he may direct his thought—currents? The occultists manifesting the greatest degree of Mental Influence acquire by practice this art of creating

Mental Images of that which they wish to materialize. They train their Imagination in this way until the very act of creating the Mental Image acts strongly toward the actual material—ization or event, as 'actually existing' in their minds before they attempt to concentrate their Thought—Waves upon the task of accomplishing it. Then the Mental Picture, being completed and standing in strong outline, they focus their mental force through it, just as in the case of the magic lantern before referred to, and the picture is reproduced on the screen of mentality of other people.

The imagination may be strengthened in many ways, the principle being constant and persistent practice. The practice of recalling to the memory of scenes previously witnessed, and then whether describing them to others or else drawing a rough picture of them will help in this matter. Describe to others scenes that you have witnessed, occurrences, details of appearances, etc. etc., until you are able to reproduce mentally the aspects and appearances of the things. Then you may begin to draw mental pictures of things desired as if they were being drawn on the screen of your mind. See, mentally, the things as actually occurring—create a little playhouse of your own, in your mind, and there enact the plays that you wish to witness in actual life. When you have acquired this, you will be able to project your mental pictures on the screen of objectivity in actual life with far greater effect.

In thinking of this subject, you would do well to remember the illustration of the magic lantern, for the figure is a good one, and will enable you to carry the idea better in your mind. You see, in giving you this suggestion, we are really telling you to form a mental picture of the mental magic lantern, using the illustration given—you see how much easier it is for you to think of it in this way and how much easier it is for you to manifest it in practice.

Build your Mental Images by degrees, commencing with the general outlines, and then filling in the details. Always commence by trying simple and easy things, and then working up to the more complex and difficult feats.

And now, I offer a word of warning at this point to all. Do not allow your imagination to 'run away with you'—do not became a dreamer of dreams and a doer of nothing. You must master your imagination and make it your servant and not your master. You must make it do your bidding, instead of allowing it to dictate to you.

You will see in the succeeding chapters the important part that Mental Imaging plays in the different phases of Mental Influence. Even when we do not refer directly to it by name, you will see that the 'idea' sought to be conveyed by one mind to another—the feeling, desire or mental state sought to be transferred from one mind to others—must and does depend very materially for strength upon the dearness and completeness of the Mental Image held in the mind of the person seeking to do the influencing, the 'projector' of the Mental Image of his mental magic lantern, upon the screen of the minds of others. Carry this principle well in mind that you may see its operation in the different forms.

CHAPTER 6

FASCINATION

In this and the next chapter we shall present to you information regarding the effect of Mental Influence manifested when there is personal contact between the persons using the power and the person affected. Then we shall pass on to a consideration of the effect produced when the persons are not in direct contact with each other.

There are two general forms of the direct use of Mental Influence, which, although somewhat resembling each other, may still be separated into two classes. The first we shall call 'Fascination' and the second 'Hypnotism.' By Fascination we mean the manifestation of Mental Influence when the two persons are together, without passes or the usual hypnotic methods. By Hypnotism we mean the use of the power, also, when the two parties are together, but accompanied by passes or hypnotic methods.

Under the head of Fascination are to be found the manifestations generally known as 'Personal Magnetism,' 'Charming,' etc., is quite commonly employed, in varying degrees by many persons, often without their conscious knowledge of the principles employed. Many persons are possessed of the power of Fascination 'naturally' and without having studied or practiced the principles. Many others, not originally possessing the power, have acquired by study and practice the power to influence people in this way. For, it must be known, the power may be acquired by study and practice just as may any other power of mind and body. To some it is easy, to others difficult—but all may acquire a very great degree of the power by intelligent study and practice of the underlying principles.

Fascination is one of the oldest forms of the manifestations of Mental Influence. It was known to, and employed by, the earliest races of men. It is even found among the lower animals that pursue their prey or capture their mates by its use. A recent writer on the subject has defined the word, used in this connection, as: 'Acting upon by some powerful or irresistible influence; influencing by an irresistible charm; alluring, exciting, irresistibly or powerfully, charming, captivating or attracting powerfully, influencing the imagination, reason or will of another in an uncontrollable manner; enchanting, captivating or alluring, powerfully or irresistibly.' As we have just said, this power is observable even among the lower animals in some cases. Instances are related by naturalists, which scorpions have fascinated other insects, causing them to circle around and around until finally the insect would plunge down right within striking distance of the scorpion, which would then devour its prey. Birds of prey unquestionably fascinate their game, and men who have been brought in contact with wild tigers, lions, etc., have testified that they felt paralyzed in some manner, their legs refusing to obey their will, and their minds seeming to become numbed and stunned. Those who have seen a mouse in the presence of a cat will testify to the effect of some power exerted by the latter. Birds in the presence of a cat and serpents also manifest symptoms of a conquered will. And naturalists cite many instances of the employment of this force by birds seeking to captivate and charm their mates at the beginning of the season.

Among men it has been noticed that certain individuals possess this power to a great degree. Some of the 'great men' of ancient and modem times having been so filled with the power that they could manage their followers almost as one would move automatons. Julius Caesar had this power developed to a great degree, and used it from youth to his last days. He was worshipped—almost as a god by his soldiers—who would undertake almost any task at his bidding. Napoleon also possessed this charm to a wonderful degree. It enabled him to control men with whom he came in contact, and to bend them to his will. He rose from a poor student to the dignity and power of the Emperor of France. When banished to Elba he escaped, and landing in France, alone and unarmed, confronted the ranks of the French army drawn up to capture him, and walking towards the soldiers compelled the latter to throw down their guns and flock to his support. He entered Paris at the head of the great army, which had been sent forth to capture him. This is no wild legend, but a sober fact of history. And in our own times we see how certain leaders of men sweep people before them and move them around like pawns on the chessboard of life.

All of the above mentioned phenomena comes under the head of Fascination, and is the result of the emanation of streams of active Thought—Waves from the mind of a person, the same being strongly concentrated and directed toward those whom the person wishes to affect. The person forms a strong thought in his mind and sends it out to the others charged with the force of concentrated will, so that the other person feels it most strongly and forcibly. The fundamental idea is the forming of the thought, and then sending it out to the other person.

For instance, if you wish a person to like you, you should form in your mind this thought: 'That person likes me,' fixing it in your own mind as a fact. Then project to him the concentrated thought, 'You like me—you like me very much,' with an air of assurance and confidence, and the other person is bound to feel the effect unless he or she has acquired a knowledge of the subject and is using self—protection. The thought should be sent forth with the strength that usually accompanies a strong spoken statement, but you must not actually 'speak' the words aloud—you should merely say them strongly 'in your mind.' If you wish to produce an effect or impress Strength upon another person, the same process may be used, changing the Thought and vibrations to the idea that you have a stronger Will than the other person, and are able to overcome his Will—using the silent message of 'I am Stronger than you—my Will overcomes yours,' Some successful agents and salesmen use the following method in reaching their customers.

They fonn a thought that the other person desires their goods very much, and then they send out the Thought—Waves that 'You desire my goods—you want them very much—you have an irresistible longing for them,' etc.

Others use the following when they wish another to comply with their wishes: 'You will do as I say—will do as I say—you will yield to me fully and completely,' etc.

You will readily see from the above examples that the whole principle employed in any and all of these cases consists of: (1) The Thought of what the person wishes the other to do held firmly in the mind; and (2) The projection of that Thought to the other, silently, in the shape of unspoken words.

In the above you have the whole secret of Fascination condensed to a small space. You will understand of course, that the words are only a means of concentrating and vitalizing the thought.

Animals merely feel Desires, but are able to fascinate by the strength of them, although they cannot use words. And one person may fascinate another without understanding a word of his language, the real strength coming from the strength of the desire behind the words. The formation of the desire—thought into words, is merely for the purpose of concentrating and focusing the thought, for words are concentrated symbols of ideas, thoughts or feelings.

The exact process of 'sending forth' the Thought—Wave to the other is difficult to describe. You know how you feel when you say something very forcible and emphatic to another person. You can fairly 'feel' the force of the words being hurled at the other person. Well, cultivate that same power in sending forth the 'unspoken word' in the above manner, and you will soon be able to notice the effect of the thought on the other. It may help you to imagine that you can see the force flying from you to the other. The imagination properly used helps very much in these matters, for it creates a mental path over which the force may travel.

You must not act awkwardly when sending out the Thought—Waves, but converse in an ordinary manner, sending your Thought—Waves between your speeches, when the other person is talking to you, or at any pause in the conversation. It is always well to send first a powerful Thought—Wave before the conversation is opened, preferably while you are approaching the person. And it is likewise well to terminate the interview with a 'parting shot' of considerable strength. You will find that these Thought—Waves are of far greater power than spoken words, and then again, you can in this way send out impressions that you could not utter in spoken words for obvious reasons.

And now do you see how you have been affected by persons who have influenced you at times in your past life? Now that you know the secret you will be in a measure immune from further impressions from others. And when you read our concluding chapter, entitled 'Self—Protection,' you will be able to surround yourself with a protective armor through which the Thought—Waves cannot penetrate, but which will turn aside the shafts directed toward you.

CHAPTER 7

HYPNOTIC INFLUENCE

As we have mentioned in the previous lesson, there is a general resemblance between the manifestation of Mental Influence, known as 'Fascination,' and that known as Hypnotic Influence. In the manifestation known as Fascination, the influence is exerted solely by Thought—Waves passing from mind to mind without a physical medium or channel other than the ether. In Hypnotic Influence, on the contrary, the influence is heightened by means of passes, stroking or eye influence.

In Hypnotic Influence the mind of the person affected, whom we shall call the 'subject,' is rendered passive by a flow of mental energy calculated to render it more or less drowsy or sleepy, and therefore less calculated to set up powers of resistance to the Thought—Waves of the person using the influence. But the power employed is the same in all cases, no matter whether they fall under the classification of Fascination or whether that of Hypnotic Influence. The two classes of manifestation, as a matter of fact, really blend into each other, and it is difficult to draw a dividing line in some cases.

Hypnotic Influence is a form of that which was formerly termed Mesmerism, which name was given to it in honor of its discoverer, Frederick Anton Mesmer, who practiced this form of Mental Influence during the latter half of the Eighteenth Century. As a fact, however, the force and its use was known to the ancients centuries before Mesmer's time, the latter person having merely rediscovered it.

Mesmer taught that the power was based upon the presence of a strange universal fluid which pervaded everything, and which had a peculiar effect upon the nerves and brains of people. He and his followers believed that it was necessary to put the subjects into a sound sleep before they could be influenced. But both of these ideas have given way to the new theories on the subject now held by investigators and students of the subject.

It is now known that the 'magnetic fluid' believed in by Mesmer and his followers is nothing else than the currents of Thought—Waves emanating from the mind of the operator. And it is also known that the 'deep sleep' condition is not necessary to render the will of the subject subservient to that of the operator. It is also now known that the nerves of the arms and fingers afford a highly sensitive conductor for the mental currents, which may be propelled over them to the mind of the subject, or to his nerves and muscles. This fact is explained by the well—known scientific fact that the material of which the nerves are composed is almost identical with that of the brain—in fact the nervous system may be spoken of as a continuation of the brain itself. It is now also known that the eye has a peculiar property of transmitting the mental currents along the rays of light entering it and from thence to the eyes of the other person. The above fact explains the phenomena of hypnotic influence, as it is now known to science. The question of 'Suggestion' also has a bearing on the subject, as we shall see presently.

Modem operators do not produce the 'deep sleep' condition usually except in cases when it is desired to produce some form of psychic phenomena apart from the subject of Mental Influence—that is, in which they are merely inducing the deep hypnotic condition in order to get the subject into a psychic condition in which the phenomena mentioned may be manifested or exhibited. We shall not enter into this phase of the subject in this book, for it is outside of the immediate subject.

The modem hypnotic investigator merely induces a passive state in the mind, nerves or muscles of the subject sufficient to reduce the powers of resistance, and then he gives his orders or 'verbal suggestions' accompanied by a projection of his Thought—Waves into the mind of the subject.

In order to illustrate the subject, we will give you a few experiments, which may be easily performed by anyone manifesting the power of concentration and thought—projection. There is of course a great difference in the degrees of impressionability of different persons to hypnotic influence—that is to say, difference in degrees of resistance. Some persons will interpose a strong resistance, while others will set up a very feeble resistance, which is easily beaten down by the will of the operator. In the following experiments you had better begin by getting some person who is perfectly willing for the experiment, and who will not interpose a resistance but who is willing to become passive. Some person friendly to you and interested in the experiments, we mean.

Begin by having the person stand before you. Then make sweeping passes in front of the person from head to foot. Then make a few passes in front of the face of the subject, then along his arms.

Then take hold of his hands and hold them a little while, looking him straight in the eyes. Make all passes downward. Avoid levity or laughter and maintain a serious, earnest expression and frame of mind.

Then standing in front of the subject tell him to take his will off of his legs and stand perfectly passive and relaxed. Then looking him straight in the eyes, say to him: 'Now, I am going to draw you forward toward me by my mental power—you will feel yourself falling forward toward me—don't resist but let yourself come toward me—I will catch you, don't be afraid—now come—come—come—now you're coming, that's right,' etc. You will find that he will begin to sway toward you and in a moment or two will fall forward in your arms. It is unnecessary to say that you should concentrate your mind steadily upon the idea of his falling forward, using your will firmly to that effect. It will help matters if you hold your hands on each side of his head, but just in front of him, not touching him, however, and then draw away your hands, toward yourself, saying at the same time: 'Come now come—you're coming,' etc. Standing behind the subject and drawing him backward may reverse this experiment. Be sure and catch him in your arms when he fails to protect him from a fall to the floor.

In the same manner you may fasten his hands together, telling him that he cannot draw them apart. Or you may start him revolving his hands, and then giving him orders that he cannot stop them. Or you may draw him all around the room after you, following your finger that you have pointed at his nose. Or you may make him experience a feeling of heat and pain by touching your finger to his hand and telling him that it is hot. All of the familiar simple experiments may be performed successfully upon a large percentage of persons, in this way, by following the above general directions. We shall not go into detail of the higher experiments of Hypnotism, as that forms a special subject by itself. We give the above experiments merely for the purpose of showing you that the phenomena of Hypnotic Influence does not require any 'magnetic fluid' theory, and is all explainable upon the hypothesis of Mental Influence by means of Thought—Waves and Mental Induction.

In the above experiments, be sure you 'take off' the influence afterward, by making upward passes, and willing that the influence pass off. Do not neglect this.

In your experiments, if you care to undertake them, you will soon discover the power of your eye upon the other persons. You will be able to almost feel the force passing from your gaze to theirs. And this is true in the case of the passes and stroking of the hands. You will feel the vibratory waves flowing from your hands into their nervous system. It is wonderful what power is aroused in a person after conducting a few experiments along these lines. Those who care to follow the subject further are referred to a forthcoming book of this series, to be issued shortly, and which will be called 'The New Hypnotism,' in which full instructions will be given in the higher phenomena, in complete detail.

And now a word of warning—Beware of people who are always putting their hands on you, or patting or stroking you, or wishing to hold your hands a long time. Many persons do this from force of habit, and innocently, but others do so with the intention of producing a mild form of hypnotic influence upon you. If you meet such persons, and find them attempting anything of this sort, you can counteract their influence by sending them a strong thought current (as stated in our last chapter), sending them the thought: 'You can't affect me—I am too strong for you—you can't play your tricks on me.' It is a good plan to practice this counteracting force when you are shaking hands with a 'magnetic' person who seems to affect people. You will soon be able to distinguish these people by a certain force about them and a peculiar expression in their eyes, at the same time using your protective will upon them.

Caution young girls against allowing young men to be too free in using their hands in caressing them, and a word of advice to young men in your family would not be out of place in this respect.

There are many cases of sex—attraction, leading to very deplorable results, arising from a conscious or unconscious use of this simple form of Hypnotic Influence. The danger lies in the fact that it renders one passive to other influences, and more readily led into temptation and to yield to the desires or will of the other person. A word to the wise should be sufficient. The use of this power for immoral purposes is a terrible crime and brings down upon the user deplorable results, which all occultists know and teach. Everyone should learn to resist such influences when exerted upon them. Forewarned is Forearmed.

CHAPTER 8

INFLUENCING AT A DISTANCE

In the two preceding chapters we invited your consideration of the manifestation of Mental Influence when the user or projector of the force was in actual contact with, or in presence of, the person or persons he was aiming to influence. In this chapter, and the one immediately following it, we shall pass on to a consideration of the manifestation of the influence when the persons affected are removed in space from the person using the influence.

The general public is familiar in a general way with the phenomena of hypnotism, and to a lesser degree with the phenomena of Fascination in its more common forms of personal Magnetism, etc.

But as regards the use of the influence at a distance people are more or less skeptical owing to a lack of knowledge of the subject. And still every day is bringing to the mind of the public new facts and instances of such an influence, and the teaching of various cults along these lines is now awakening a new interest in the subject, and a desire to learn something regarding the laws and principles underlying the same.

As strange as it may appear at first glance, the principles underlying Mental Influence at a distance are precisely the same as those underlying the use of influence when the persons are in the presence of each other. A little thought must show the truth of this. In the case of present influence the mental—currents flow across an intervening space between the two minds—there is a space outside of the two minds to be traversed by the currents And a moment's thought will show you that the difference between present influence and distant influence is merely a matter of degree—a question of a little more or less space to be traversed by the currents. Do you see this plainly? Well, then, this being so, it follows that the methods used must be identical. Of course, in the case of personal influence the added effect of the voice, manner, suggestive methods, the eye, etc., are present, which render the result more easily obtained, and causes the 'rapport' condition to be more easily established. But with this exception the methods are identical, and even the advantages accruing from the exception mentioned may be duplicated by practice and development in the case of distant influence.

There are a number of methods given by the authorities in this matter of distant influencing, but they are all based upon the same principles named in the previous chapters of this book, i.e. Vibrations, Thought—Waves, Mental Induction, Concentration and Mental Imaging—in these words you have the key to the subject—the rest is all a matter of practice and development, and variation.

One of the most elementary, and yet one of the most effective methods known to occultists is that of creating a Mental Image of the person 'treated' (for that is the common term among modem writers on the subject) in the sense of imagining him to be seated in a chair in front of the person treating him at a distance. The treater proceeds to give both verbal commands, and at the same time directs Thought—Waves toward the imaginary person seated before him. This process establishes a psychic condition between the treator and the actual person, although the latter may be removed from the treator by many miles of space. This was the method of the ancient magicians and wonder—workers, and has always been a favorite among persons pursuing these experiments, of desirous, of mentally influencing others at a distance.

A variation of the above, very common in former days, was to mold a clay or wax figure, calling it by the name of the person treated, and identifying it in the mind and imagination with the other person. A variation is also noticed in the cases where a photograph, lock of hair, article of clothing, etc., is used in this way as a psychic connecting link between the two persons. The practitioners of Black Magic, Witchcraft and of her nefarious perversions of Mental influence seemed to prefer these methods, although, on the contrary, they are used with the very best results today by many in giving beneficial treatments to absent patients, friends and others whose welfare is desired. The only effect the Mental Image of the person, or the picture, etc., has is the fact that by these means a psychic connection link is set up along which the Thought—Waves travel more readily.

In the above forms of treatment the treator treats the Mental Image, picture, etc., precisely as he would if the person were actually present. He forgets for the time being that the person may be hundreds of miles away, and concentrates his influence on the image, or picture, etc., because the latter is really the starting point of the psychic chain, which leads direct to the person. The treator sends his Thought—Waves toward the object, and in some cases actually talks (mentally) to the person by means of the medium mentioned. He may give commands, arguments, remonstrance, persuasion, etc., just as if the person were actually present. In short, he acts as if the person were sitting before him, wide—awake, and receptive to his influence.

Another way, employed by some, is to begin darting Thought—Waves toward the other person, forming in the imagination a gradual lengthening 'psychic—wire' composed of thought—vibrations. Those practicing this form state that when the psychic—wire is projected sufficiently far (and it travels with incredible speed) and comes in contact with the mind of the other person, the treator feels at once that contact has been established by a peculiar faint 'shock' similar to that of a very mild galvanic current. Then the treator proceeds to send his thought currents along the psychic—wire in the same manner as if the person were actually in his presence, as described under the head of 'Fascination, in a preceding chapter. In fact, such treatments, and the others mentioned in this chapter, are really and practically 'long distance Fascination.' Another form of distant treatment consists in forming an 'astral—tube,' mentioned in other books in this series. The astral—tube is set up in a similar manner to the 'psychic—wire,' and projected toward the person desired to influence. It is formed in the imagination as a 'vortex—ring,' similar to the little ring of smoke puffed out by the cigar smoker, only larger—about six inches to one foot wide—or, better still, like the ring of smoke ejected from the stack of a locomotive sometimes when it is puffing rapidly. This vortex—ring is then seen, in the imagination, by the use of the will, to lengthen out in the shape of a tube which rapidly extends and travels toward the person treated, in a manner identical with that of the psychic—wire. This tube is known to occultists as the 'astral—tube,' and is employed in various forms of occult and psychic phenomena, such as clairvoyance and other forms of 'Psychomancy,' as described by us in our volume of this series, so entitled. Those following this method of distant influencing report that they recognize the completion of the tube by a sensation of stoppage and a feeling of 'rapport' having been established between themselves and the other person. In some cases they report that they are able to faintly 'see' the figure of the other person in miniature at the other end of the tube, but this is undoubtedly due to the possession of 'psycho—mantic' powers, suddenly awakened in to effect. The tube once established the treatment is proceeded with as if they were in the actual presence of the person treated. In many respects the 'psychic—wire' and the 'astral—tube' methods are similar, and a statement concerning one is generally true of the other. There are two other methods frequently used in distant influencing which we shall now briefly describe.

The first of these two methods consists in sitting or standing in a quiet place, or rather in some place in which you can concentrate (the advanced occultist can find peace in the midst of the noise) and then directing your Thought—Waves toward the other person, forming in the imagination a mental picture of the force flying from you toward the other, like tiny sparks of electricity, or of a subtle fluid. This mental picture tends to give a concentrative force to the current, which renders them powerful, and sends them direct to the desired spot.

The second of these two methods is that used by the most advanced occultists who have advanced beyond the use of the methods described just now. These people simply stand or sit quietly and concentrate their minds until they attain the state of Mental Calm known to many as 'the Silence.' Then they create a strong mental picture of the person treated, surrounded by the conditions desired created, or doing the things desired to be done. This is one of the highest forms of Mental Influence and really approaches a higher phase of influence than that of the mental plane as generally known. A picture of a person held in the mind in this way—the person being seen in perfect, robust health, and happy and successful tends to materialize the same conditions in the person in real life. This form of treatment, however, is possible only to those of great concentration, and who have mastered the act of Mental Imaging, and who also possess Creative Will—Power to a marked degree. Some degree of success in it, however, is open to nearly every student who practices along these lines.

Before practicing any of these experiments, read what we have said in the chapter on 'Magic Black and White, and guard against employing the power for evil purposes, for the fate of the Black Magician is a sad one.

CHAPTER 9

INFLUENCING 'EN MASSE'

In our last chapter we considered the manifestation of Mental Influence at a distance in so far as was concerned the influencing of one or more persons by another. There is another phase of the subject that must not be overlooked, and that is the influencing of large numbers of people by some active, strong projector of Mental Influence. This form of the manifestation of the power is known as 'Mental Influencing En Masse'—'En Masse, of course, means 'in a body'—or 'in a crowd,' and Mental Influencing En Masse means the use of the influence in the phase of exerting a strong attracting or directing power to the mind of 'the crowd,' or rather, 'the public, or a large number of people.

This form of the use of the power is that consciously or unconsciously exerted by the great leaders of men in the fields of statesmanship, politics, business, finance or military life. You will at once recall a number of the so called 'great men' of history from ancient times down to our own times who seemed to exert a wonderfully, almost miraculous, effect upon the minds of the people, causing men to see things through the eyes of the strong man, and making of all instruments to cany out the ideals, will or desires of these great masters of Mental Influence. And on a smaller scale are the majority of the successful people who depend upon public support. In fact, this influence in some degree is used by nearly all who succeed in any form of business or profession, in which success calls for the attraction of other people toward the occupation of the person in question. This may seem like a strange thought to many, but occultists know it as the truth, notwithstanding.

The most common form of Influencing En Masse is the lesser degree manifestation, along unconscious lines, manifested by a majority of people by reason of their desire for the success of certain things. By desire we do not mean the mere 'wanting' or 'wishing' state of mind, but rather that eager longing, craving, demanding mental state that evinces a hungry reaching out for the desired thing. You will notice that the men and women who 'get things' are generally those who are possessed of a strong, burning desire for the things in question, which prompts them to be more of less aggressive in the search for satisfaction of the desire possessing them. These people are constantly sending out strong waves of thought—vibrations, which has a drawing, attracting influence upon all with whom they come in contact, and tending to draw such persons toward the center of attraction, which is, of course, the mind of the person sending out such thoughts. And in the same way a person possessed of a strong Fear of a thing will send out similar attracting waves, which have a tendency to attract or draw to him the people calculated to bring about the materialization of the thing feared. This may sound paradoxical, but the secret lies in the fact that in both the case of Desire and Fear the mind forms the Mental Image, which tends to become materialized. Fear, after all, is a form of 'expectation,' which, alas, too, often tends to materialize it.' The thing that I have feared, hath come upon me,' says Job, and in that saying he has stated the experience of the race. The way to fight things you may fear is to create a burning desire for the opposite thing.

Other persons who have either studied the principles of Mental Influence, or else have stumbled upon certain facts concerning the same, improve upon this elementary form of Influencing En Masse just mentioned. They send out the Thought—Waves consciously and deliberately, erecting the mental image, and holding strongly to it, so that in time theirs weeps of mental currents reach further and further away and bring a greater number of people under the influence and into the field of attraction. They 'treat' the public 'en masse' by holding the strong mental picture of that which they desire, and then sending out strong thought—currents of desire in all directions, willing that those coming within their radius shall be attracted toward the ideas expressed in the Mental image projected in all directions.

The constant dwelling upon some special object or subject, by men who have developed concentration, strong wills and fixity of purpose, has the effect of sending out from the mind of that person great circles, constantly widening, of Thought—Waves, which sweep ever outward like waves in a pond caused by dropping in a stone. These waves reach and affect a great number of people, and will render them at least 'interested' in the object or subject thought of, and the indifference has been overcome. Other appeals to the minds of these people will be far more likely to reach them than otherwise, for 'interest' is the first step toward attention, and attention is another step toward action.

Of course, there are very many people sending out circles of Thought—Waves, and these currents come in contact with each other and tend to neutralize each. But now and then a particularly strong man will send out waves that will persist even after meeting other currents, and will reach the minds of the public in spite of the opposition. These thought—currents have the personality of the sender, and reflect the character of his will, be it strong or weak. The Mental Influence sent out by a strong business man in a town will soon make itself felt in a subtle manner, and the store becomes a center of attractive influence, although the public does no understand just why. In the same way some lawyers spring into public favor, although not possessing greater ability than their legal brethren. And popular preachers make their influence felt in a community in similar ways, although often they are not conscious of just what force they are using, their only knowledge being that they have a feeling of inward strength and an attractive influence over people, and at the same time a burning ardent desire to draw people their way, and a strong will to back it up with. And these are just the mental qualities that create and manifest the strongest kind of Mental Influence. And besides, these people almost invariably 'know just what they want'—there is no mere vague 'wishing' about them—they make a clear mental picture of the things that they wish to bring about, and then they bend every effort toward materializing the picture. Everything they do towards accomplishing their ends gives an additional impetus to their constantly widening and constantly strengthening circle of power and influence.

Some masters of this art of influencing the public create a mental picture of themselves sending out great volumes of Thought—Waves for a time, and then afterward mentally imparting a rotary motion to the waves, until at last they form a mental whirlpool rushing round and round and always sucking in toward the center. An effort of this kind acts on the mental plane just as a physical whirlpool acts on the physical plane, that is it draws into its power all that comes in contact with its force. This is one of the most powerful forms of Influencing En Masse, and is used with great effect by many of the 'strong men' of this age; who have acquainted themselves fully with the secrets of the ancient occultists. Ancient Occultism and Modem Finance seem far apart, but they are really working together to further the interests of some of these powerful minds of the day—and the public is paying the bill.

You will readily see from what has been said that an individual who has cultivated the faculty of concentration and has acquired the art of creating sharp, clear, strong mental images, and who when engaged in an undertaking will so charge his mind with the idea of success, will be bound to become an attracting center. And if such an individual will keep his mental picture ever in his mind, even though it may be in the background of his mind, when he is attending to the details and planning of his affairs—if he will give his mental picture a prominent place in his mental gallery, taking a frequent glance at it, and using his will upon it to create new scenes of actual success, he will create for himself a center of radiating thought that will surely be felt by those coming within its field of influence.

Such a man frequently 'sees' people coming to him and his enterprises and falling in line with his plans. He mentally 'sees' money flowing in to him, and all of his plans working out right. In short, he mentally imagines each step of his plans a little ahead of the time for their execution and he concentrates forcibly and earnestly upon them. It is astonishing to witness how events, people, circumstances and things seem to move in place in actual life as if urged by some mighty power to serve to materialize the conditions so imaged in the mind of the man. But, understood, there has got to be active mental effort behind the imaging. Daydreamers do not materialize thought—they merely dissipate energy. The man who converts thought in activity and material being, throws energy into the task and puts forth his willpower through the picture on the slide. Without the rays of the will there will be no picture projected, no matter how beautifully the imagination has pictured it. Thoughts pictured in mental images and then vitalized by the force of the desire and will tend to objectify themselves into material beings, That is the whole thing in a nutshell.

CHAPTER 10

THE NEED OF KNOWLEDGE

Although the true scientific principles underlying the subject of Mental Influence have been but recently recognized and taught to the general public, still the knowledge is far from being new. The occultists of the old civilizations undoubtedly understood the underlying principles and used them in practice, thus gaining an ascendancy over the masses. And more than this, the masses themselves had a more or less comprehensive knowledge of the working principles of the subject, for we find among all peoples, in all times, records of the use of this power. Under one name or another—under one form or another—Mental Influence has been operated and used from the earliest times. And today, even in the most remote portions of the globe, and among the most savage and barbarous races we find instances of the employment of this force.

The forms of the manifestation of Mental Influence are many and varied. In some cases it manifests under the form of a fascinating, attracting power exerted by some people, which causes such persons to draw or attract other persons to them. Persons are allured or 'charmed' by others possessing this power, and their affections are taken captive by this mysterious force. Some persons are spoken of as 'fascinating,' 'possessing powers of charming,' having 'winning ways,' having 'great personal magnetism,' etc. Others exert another form of the power in the driving of and compelling others to do their bidding, and people speak of them as having 'a compelling will,' being able 'to work their will' on those around them, possessing 'dominating powers,' etc. We are also brought face to face with the wonderful effects of 'Mental Science' under one form or another, under this name or that term, with the many forms of 'treatments' followed by the different schools and cults. Then we read in the pages of history about the mysterious powers recorded under the name of Witchcraft, Hexes, Voodoo's, and Black Magic, including the Hawaiian 'Kahuna' work. And turning back the pages of history to Ancient time, Greece, Persia and Egypt, not to speak of India, ancient and modem, we find innumerable instances of the employment of, and knowledge of, Mental influence in some of its forms.

And although many will seek to deny the fact, scientific investigators and students realize that there is but one real underlying principle under and back of all of the various forms of manifestation. The good results, and the evil results, all arise from the employment of the same force, strange as it may appear at first thought. The secret lies in the fact that this Mental Influence is a great natural force, just as is electricity or any other natural forces, and it may be, and is, used for both good and evil purposes. The electricity which runs out machines, lights our houses and performs countless other beneficent tasks in the service of man is also used to electrocute criminals, and the unfortunate person who touches a 'live wire' may be struck with instant death. The sun, which warms our earth and renders life possible, also kills countless persons exposed to its rays on the desert, or even in our large cities. Fire, that great friend of man, which has been one of the most potent factors in the evolution of the race from barbarism to civilization, is also a mighty enemy, destroying both property and lives. Water, that most necessary element, which renders life possible, and which is necessary to grow our grain and to perform countless other good services for us, also acts as an enemy at times, drowning people and sweeping away their homes. Gravitation, which holds all things in place, from suns and stars down to the tiniest atom of matter, also causes people to fall to their death from high places, or brings down on their heads objects from above them. In short, every natural force or power is capable of producing cither beneficent or baleful effects to man, according to the circumstances of the case. We recognize these things, and accept them as a law of nature. And yet some would deny the identity of the power of Mental influence as manifested in its good and bad uses.

There be people who ascribe to God all the good qualities of Mental Influence, and ascribe to the Devil all of its evil uses. These people have primitive minds. Their counterparts are seen in those who would credit God with the helpful rain or sun, and who ascribe to the Devil the same things when there occurs a flood or a drought. Such reasoning is worthy only of the savage mind. The forces are natural forces, and work according to their own laws, imminent in their constituent qualities and nature, and are in that sense 'above good and evil.' When they work for man's interest and comfort man calls them 'good'—when they work harm and discomfort to him man call them 'bad'. And thus it is with the power of Mental Influence—it is above 'good' and 'bad' in itself—it is a great natural force, capable of being used for either weal or woe to mankind.

But, remember this, there is a difference. While the force in itself is neither good nor bad the individual who employs it may be, and it is, 'good' or 'bad,' according to its use. Just as a man commits a good or bad act when he uses his gun to slay a wild beast attacking another man, or else turns it upon his brother or neighbor, as the case may be—so is a man good or bad according to his use of Mental Influence. The merit or demerit lies in the intention and purpose of the user, not in the force or power employed by him. Therein lies the difference.

On all sides of us we may see the manifestation of the possession of Mental Influence. We see men who are able to sway those around them in some mysterious and wonderful way, either by their powers of persuasion of by their dominant will power. Some spring into prominence and power suddenly, in a way unaccountable to those who are ignorant of the secret of Mental Influence. As we have said in a previous chapter, certain

people seem to have 'something about them' that makes them attractive or successful in their relations with other people. The 'personal magnetism' of leaders manifests itself strongly, some having this power to such an extent that the masses follow them like a great flock of sheep after the 'bell—whether' with the tinkling bell around his neck.

We have all come in contact with the 'agent' or salesman who managed in some way to sell us things that we did not want and had no use for, and after he had gone we wondered and wondered how it all happened. If we had but understood the laws of Mental Influence this could not have happened. We have all felt ourselves, at some time or another in our lives, in the presence of individuals who almost compelled us to do what we knew in our hearts we should not do. Knowledge of the laws of Mental influence would have enabled us to overcome the temptation.

And not only in the case of personal interviews have we been affected. There is a far more subtle and dangerous use of the power, i.e., in the shape of 'distant influence,' or 'absent treatment,' as it had been called. And the increase in the interest and knowledge of Occult matters during the past twenty years has resulted in a widely diffused knowledge of this great force, and its consequent employment, worthily and unworthily, by many people who are thereby enabled to gain an influence over their neighbors and fellow men, who are not familiar with the laws of the force. It would surprise many people if they knew that some of the multi—millionaires of the country, and some of its greatest politicians and leaders, were secret students of Occultism, and who were using their forces upon the masses of the people.

Not only this, but there are Schools of Occultism which teach their pupils the theory, practice and art of Mental Influence, under one name or another—under this guise or that—the result being that there are a greater number of people equipped for the use of this force and instructed in the practice of employing it turned out every year than is generally imagined. There are Schools for Salesmanship giving disguised instruction in theart of Mental Influence. Nearly every large concern employing selling agents has private instructors for their men, who teach them the principles of Mental Influence disguised under the name of 'Psychology of Business,' or some such name.

And besides these, there are a number of people who have studied at the feet of some of the great metaphysical, semi—religious cults of the day, who have received instruction in Mental influence disguised under the name of some creed or religious teachings, who have departed from the moral principles inculcated by their by their teachers, and who are using their knowledge in the shape of 'treatments' of other persons for the purpose of influencing them to accede to their wishes or to act so as to bring financial gain to the person giving the treatment. The air is full of this Black Magic today, and it is surely time that the general masses were instructed on this subject. And this is the purpose of this little book, published and sold at a popular price in order to bring it within the reach of the purses of the 'plain people,' who have been exploited and influenced by those who have acquired a knowledge of the principles of Mental Influence, and who are using it unworthily upon their fellow men.

There is self protection possible to all, and this little book purposes to teach you how to use it.

CHAPTER 11

MAGIC BLACK AND WHITE

The use of the word 'Magic' in connection with Mental Influence is quite ancient. Occultists make a clear distinction between the use of Mental Influence in a manner conducive to the welfare of others, and its use in a selfish, base manner calculated to work harm on others. Both forms are common and are frequently mentioned in all occult writings.

White Magic has many forms, both in its ancient manifestations and in these latter days of revived occult knowledge. The use of Mental Influence in this way generally takes the form of kindly 'treatments' of persons by others having their welfare at heart. In this particular class fall the various treatments of the several cults and schools of what is known as Mental Science, or similar names. These people make a practice of giving treatments, both 'present' and 'absent,' for the purpose of healing physical ailments and bringing about a normal Physical condition of health and strength. Similar treatments are given by some to bring about a condition of Success to others, by imparting to the minds of such persons the vibrations of courage, confidence, energy, etc., which surely make for success along the lines of material occupation, etc.

In the same way one may 'treat' adverse conditions surrounding others, bringing the force of the mind and will to bear on these conditions with the idea of changing the prevailing vibrations and bringing harmony from in—harmony, and success from failure.

The majority of persons, not informed along these lines, are surrounded by a mental atmosphere arising from the prevailing mental states, thoughts, feelings, etc., and also arising from the thought—currents which they have attracted to them by the Law of Mental Attraction. These Mental Atmospheres, when once firmly settled around a person, render it most difficult for him to 'break away' from their vibrations. He struggles and fights, but the prevailing vibrations are beating down upon him all the time and must produce a strong effect upon even persons of strong will, unless indeed they have fully acquainted themselves with the laws of Mental influence and have acquired the power of Concentration. The habit of a lifetime, perhaps, has to be overcome, and besides the constant suggestive vibrations from the mental atmosphere are constantly bringing a pressure to bear upon the person, so that indeed he has a mighty task before him to throw off the old conditions, unaided and alone. And, so, while individual effort is preferable, there comes a time in the lives of many people when 'a helping hand,' or rather a 'helping mind,' is of great service and aid.

The person coming to the mental aid of a person needing his or her services is performing a most worthy and proper act. We hear a great deal about 'interfering with other people's minds' in such kind and worthy 'treatments,' but in many cases there is but little real interference done. The work of the helper is really in the nature of neutralizing and dissipating the unfavorable. Mental Influence surrounds the other person, and thereby giving the other person a chance to work out his own mental salvation. It is true that everyone must do his or her own work, but help of the kind above indicated is surely most worthy and proper.

In these White Magic treatments the person giving the treatments forms the Mental Picture of the desired condition in his mind, and then sends his thought—currents to the other person endeavoring to reproduce the Mental Picture in the mind or thought—atmosphere of the other person. The best way of doing this, of course, is to assert mentally that the desired condition actually exists. One may be of great help and aid to others in this way, and there is no good reason why it should not be done.

And now for the reverse side of the shield—We wish it were possible to avoid even a mention of this hateful form and manifestation of Mental Influence, but we feel that ignorance is no protection, and that it is useless and foolish to pursue the policy of the ostrich which sticks its head in the sand when pursued, that not seeing the hunter the latter may not see him. We believe that it is better to look things in the face, particularly where it is a case of 'forewarned being forearmed.' It is a fact known to all students of occultism that Black Magic has been frequently employed in all times to further the selfish, base aims of some people. And it is also known to advanced thinkers today that even in this enlightened age there are many who do not scruple to stoop to the use of this hateful practice in order to serve their own ends, notwithstanding the punishment that occultists know awaits such persons.

The annals of history are full of records of various forms of witchcraft, conjuration and similar forms of Black Magic. All the much talked of forms of 'putting spells' upon people are really forms of Black Magic, heightened by the fear and superstition of those affected.

One has but to read the history of witchcraft to see that there was undoubtedly some force at work behind all of the appalling superstition and ignorance shown by the people of those times. What they attributed to the influence of people 'in league with the devil' really arose from the use of Black Magic, or an unworthy use of Mental Influence, the two things being one. An examination of the methods used by these 'witches,' as shown by their confessions, gives us a key to the mystery. These 'witches' would fix their minds upon other people, or their animals, and by holding a concentrated mental picture there, would send forth Thought—Waves affecting the welfare of the persons being 'adversely treated,' which would influence and disturb them, and often bring on sicknesses. Of course, the effect of these 'treatments' were greatly heightened by the extreme ignorant fear and superstition held by the masses of people at the time, for Fear is ever a weakening factor in Mental influence, and the superstitions and credulity of the people caused their minds to vibrate in such a manner as to render them extremely passive to the adverse influences being directed against them.

It is well known that the Voodoos of Africa, and similar cults among other savage races, practice Black Magic among their people with great effect. Among the natives of Hawaii there are certain men known as 'Kahunas,' who pray people sick, or well, whichever way they are paid for. These instances could be multiplied had we the space and inclination to proceed further with the matter.

And in our own civilized lands there are many people who have learned the principles of Mental Influence, and who are using the same for unworthy purposes, seeking to injure others and defeat their undertakings, or else trying to bring them around to their own (the 'treator's') point of view and inclinations. The modem revival of occult knowledge has operated along two lines. On the one hand we see and hear of the mighty power for good Mental Influence is exerting among the people today, raising up the sick, strengthening the weak, putting courage into the despondent and making successes of failures. But on the other hand the hateful selfishness and greed of unprincipled persons in taking advantage of this mighty force of nature and prostituting it to their own hateful ends, without heeding the dictates of conscience or the teaching of religion or morality. These people are sowing a baleful wind that will result in their reaping a frightful whirlwind on the mental plane. They are bringing down upon themselves pain and misery in the future.

At this point we wish to utter a solemn warning to those who have been, or are tempted, to employ this mighty force for unworthy purposes .The laws of the mental plane are such that 'as one sows so shall he reap.' The mighty Law of Attraction acts with the accuracy of a machine, and those who seek to entangle others in a net of Mental influence sooner or later are caught by their own snare. The Black Magician involves him to pieces. He is sucked down into the whirlpool of his own making, and is dragged down to the lowest depths. These are not idle remarks, but a statement of certain laws of nature, in operation on the mental plane, which all should know and heed.

And to those who may feel appalled at this mention of the existence and possibilities of Black Magic we would say that there is one thing to be remembered, and that is that GOOD always overcomes EVIL on the mental plane. A good thought always has the power to neutralize the Evil one, and a person whose mind is filled with Love and Faith may combat a multitude whose minds are filled with Hate and Evil. The tendency of all nature is upward and toward Good. And he who would pull it back toward Evil sets himself against the law of Spiritual Evolution, and sooner or later falls a victim to his folly.

And then, remember this: Thought—Waves find entrance only to those minds that are accustomed to think similar thoughts. He who thinks Hate may be affected by Hate thoughts, while he whose mind is filled with Faith and Love is surrounded by a resistant armor which repels the invading waves, and causes them to be deflected, or else driven back to their senders. Bad thoughts, like chickens, come home to roost. Thoughts ace like Boomerangs, in their tendency to return to their sender. To the poison of Black Magic Nature gives the antidote of Right—Thinking.

CHAPTER 12

SELF—PROTECTION

The reader of the preceding chapters will see the power of Mental Influence in its various phases of manifestation, and will recognize the possibility of the force being used to influence himself. The question that will naturally arise in the mind of every student and investigator of this important subject, and which comes to all at sometime, is: 'How may I protect myself from the use of this power against myself—how may I render myself immune from these influences which may be directed against me?' It is true that we, and other writers on the subject, have shown you that one is far less liable to influence if he will maintain a mental atmosphere of high vibration—that is keeping oneself surrounded by a thought atmosphere filled with vibrations of the highest kind of thoughts and free from thoughts and desire of a base, selfish character, which tends to attract similar thoughts. In this way one creates a state of mental hygienic cleanliness which renders him immune from the 'contagious thoughts of the selfish plane of desire,' etc. This should be remembered and taken advantage of by everyone, for just as physical cleanliness gives no congenial lodgment for the germs of disease, so mental cleanliness refuses to admit the mental microbes.

But there is a method far more efficacious than even the above—mentioned plan. And this method is really that employed by the adepts in Occultism, and the method and practice taught the initiates of the occult brotherhoods and lodges all over the world. Let us consider it here.

In the first place, without entering into a statement of the details of the high occult teachings, we wish to inform you that the Basic Principle of all such teaching and instruction is the fact that within each of us, in the very center of the being of each individual—in the very heart of hearts of the immortal Ego—is what occultists know as the Flame of the Spirit. This is what you recognize in consciousness as the 'I AM' consciousness—that consciousness of being which is far above the consciousness of Personality, or the things of personality. It is that consciousness which informs each individual, unmistakably, that he IS actually an Individual Being. This consciousness comes to the individual by reason of his contact with the great One Life of the Universe—it is the point of contact between the PART and the ALL.

And in this part of a man's consciousness, coupled with the sense of BEING and 'I,' there resides a spark from the Divine Flame of Life and Power, which is what has been called the WILL of man. Now, do not mistake us and confuse this with the so called Will of personality, which is merely a Desire, or else a certain firmness, which often is little more than Stubbornness. This inner Will is Real Power, and when once recognized may be drawn upon as a source of unending and unfailing Strength. The occult adepts have developed the consciousness of this Power Within, and use it freely. This is the result of years of practice, and correct living and thinking. But, still, each and every person may draw upon this source of strength within them to aid them in life and to repel the thought—vibrations of the lower plane.

This consciousness may be developed by a realization of its existence, and by a practice of bringing the idea in everyday consciousness, by thought, meditation and practice. The very fact of having called your attention to its existence has awakened within the mind of You who are reading these lines a new strength and sense of power. Think a moment and see whether you do not feel a dawning sense of Strength within you that you have not realized so fully before this moment! A continued recognition in your everyday consciousness of this Something Within will develop your ability to manifest it. Particularly in an hour of need will it spring to your assistance, giving you a sense of a part of yourself crying out to you in words of encouragement: i Am Here! Be Not Afraid! '

It is very difficult to give you this method in written or printed works, but if you will enter fully into a recognition of this Inward Power you will find yourself developing a new power of resisting outside influences that will astonish you.

When you come in contact with people who are seeking to influence you in any of the ways mentioned in the preceding chapters of this book, or in others ways, you will find yourself able to defy their mental attacks by simply remembering the strength imminent in your 'I,' aided by the statement (made silently to yourself): 'I am an Immortal Spirit, using the Will within my Ego.' With this Mental Attitude you may make the slightest mental effort in the direction of throwing out from your mind vibrations, which will scatter the adverse influences in all directions, and which, if persisted in, will cause the other person to become confused and anxious to let you alone.

With this consciousness held in mind, your mental command to another, 'Let me alone—I cast off your influence by the power of my Spirit,' will act so strongly that you will be able to actually see the effect at once. If the other person is stubborn and determined to influence you by words of suggestion, coaxing, threatening, or similar methods, look him or her straight in the eyes, saying mentally 'I defy you—my inner power casts off your influence. Try this the next time that anyone attempts to influence you either verbally or by Thought—Waves and see how strong and positive you will feel, and how the efforts of the other person will fail. This sounds simple, but the little secret is worth thousands of dollars to every individual who will put it into practice.

Above all, put out of your mind all Fear of others persons. The feeling of fear prevents you from manifesting the power within you to its full extent. Cast out fear as unworthy and hurtful.

Not only the case of personal influence in the actual presence of the other person may be defeated in this way, but the same method will act equally as well in the matter of repelling the mental influence of others directed against you in the form of 'absent treatments,' etc. If you feel yourself inclining toward doing something which in your heart you feel that is not to your best interests, judged from a true standpoint, you may know that, consciously or unconsciously someone is seeking to influence you in this way. Then smile to yourself and make the statements mentioned above, or some similar one, and holding the power of the Spirit within your T firmly in you mind, send out a mental command just as you would in the case of the actual presence of the person himself or herself. You may also deny the influencing power out of existence by asserting mentally: T DENY your power to influence me—you have no such power over me—I am resting on my knowledge of Spirit and its Will within me—I deny your power out of existence.' This form of denial may be used either in the case of absent influence or personal influence. The rule is the same in all cases.

In repelling these absent influences you will at once experience a feeling of relief and strength and will be able to smile at the defeated efforts of the other person. If you feel sufficiently broad and full of love for mankind you may then 'treat' the other person for his error, sending him thoughts of Love and Knowledge with the idea of dispelling his ignorance and selfishness, and bringing him to a realization of the higher truths of life.

You will doubtless have many interesting experiences arising from thus repelling these attacks. In some cases you will find that the next time you meet the person in question he will appear confused and puzzled and ill at ease. In other cases the person will begin to manifest a new respect and regard for you, and disposed to aid you instead of trying to influence you to his way and desire. In other cases the person will still have the desire, and will endeavor to 'argue' you into doing that which he has tried to influence you into doing by Mental Influence, but his efforts will 'fall flat,' and without effect, particularly if you give him 'another dose of the assertion of the Power of the Spirit within you.

In the same way you should call upon your Higher Self for aid and strength when you feel yourself being affected by any of the great Mental Waves of feeling or emotion sweeping over the public mind, and which have a tendency to 'stampede' people into adopting certain ideas, or of following certain leaders. In such case the assertion of the 'I' within you will dissipate the influence around you, and you will find yourself standing in a center of Peace surrounded on all sides by the ocean of mental tumult and agitation which is sweeping over or circling around the place. In the same way you will be able to neutralize the unpleasant mental atmospheres of places, localities, houses, etc., and render yourself positive to and immune from the same. In short, we have given you here a recipe that may be used in any and every instance of the employment of Mental Influence. It may sound simple to you, but a little use of it will make you deem it the most important bit of practical knowledge you may possess.

CHAPTER 13

BIBLIOGRAPHY

1. *Atkinson, William Walker. Practical Mental Influence: A Course of Lessons on Mental Vibrations, Psychic Influence, Personal Magnetism, Fascination, Psychic Self-Protection, etc., etc., Containing Practical Instruction, Exercises, Directions, etc, capable of being understood, mastered and demonstrated by any person of average intelligence. Chicago, IL: Advanced Thought Publishing Co., 1908. The Lyal Book Concern, 1908.*
2. *Gray, Elisha. Nature's Miracles: Familiar Talks on Science, Vol. 2, Energy and Vibration: Energy, Sound, Heat, Light, Explosives. New York, NY: Fords, Howard & Hulbert, 1900.*
3. Flammarion, Camille. *L'inconnu: Th Unknown.* New York, NY and London, GB: Harper & Brothers Publishers, 1900.
4. Galton, Francis. 'Mental Imagery,' *Fortnightly Review,* Vol. 28, September 1880.
5. Galton, Francis. 'Mental Imagery,' *Littells Living Age,* No. 1895, October 9, 1880. Boston, MA: Littell & Co., 1880.
6. Galton, Francis. *Inquiries into Human Faculty and Its Development.* New York, NY: Macmillan and Co., 1883
7. Williams, W. Mattieu. 'Discussions in Current Science,' *Humboldt Library of Popular Science Literature,* No. 41, February, 1883. New York, NY: J. Fitzgerald, 1883.
8. Ribot, Thodule. 'Th Psychology of Attention,' Th Humboldt Library of Science, No. 112, July, 1889. New York, NY: Th Humboldt Publishing Comany, 1889.